THE
DOLLS' CLOTHES
STORYBOOK COLLECTION

CHRISTINA HARRIS

David & Charles

A DAVID & CHARLES BOOK

First published in the UK in 2004

Text, diagrams and designs Copyright © Christina Harris 2004
Photography and layout Copyright © David & Charles 2004

Distributed in North America
by F&W Publications, Inc.
4700 East Galbraith Road
Cincinnati, OH 45236
1-800-289-0963

A catalogue record for this book is available from the British Library.

ISBN 0 7153 1685 0 hardback
ISBN 0 7153 1686 9 paperback (USA only)

Printed in China by Hong Kong Graphics & Printing Ltd.
for David & Charles
Brunel House   Newton Abbot   Devon

Executive Commissioning Editor   Cheryl Brown
Desk Editor   Ame Verso
Project Editor   Joan Gubbin
Executive Art Editor   Ali Myer
Art Editor   Prudence Rogers
Production Controller   Ros Napper
Photographer   Ginette Chapman

Visit our website at www.davidandcharles.co.uk

David & Charles books are available from all good bookshops;
alternatively you can contact our Orderline on (0)1626 334555 or write
to us at FREEPOST EX2110, David & Charles Direct, Newton Abbot,
TQ12 4ZZ (no stamp required UK mainland).

Contents

Introduction

This collection of five beautiful tableaux, taken from stories everyone is familiar with, features dolls dressed in the costumes of the characters and set in a scene from the book. Most of the stories have been made into films, so even if you have not read the books, it is likely that you are still familiar with them from childhood.

You can choose from the classic fairy tale characters of Rapunzel and her Prince, or the storybook heroines of Alice from *Alice in Wonderland*, Dorothy from *The Wizard of Oz* and Anne from *Anne of Green Gables*. Each is accompanied by another character from the story ranging from the irascible Queen of Hearts, to Diana, the perfect bosom friend and Glinda, the beautiful witch who grants Dorothy's wish to return home. Margaret Mitchell's heroine, Scarlett O'Hara and the dashing Rhett Butler from *Gone with the Wind* complete the series. You can make a single individual costume to suit a particular doll, or make the pair, and maybe even have fun creating the wonderful background tableau to set them against.

The costumes come with detailed instructions for making them as well as patterns for a complete set of underclothes, hats, shoes and accessories that are accurate for the character. The clothes are made mainly on a sewing machine with hems and finishing work done by hand. Please read the Before You Begin section and the instructions right the way through before cutting out or sewing.

Before you begin

*T*hese general instructions apply to all the patterns given in this book. Dolls come in a variety of sizes but the information given here will enable you to adapt the patterns to fit your own dolls. A useful sewing kit is suggested and basic sewing instructions and stitches are described. Several of the dressmaking techniques used are common to more than one pattern and they are given here. Read them carefully and refer back to them as directed.

Fabrics

The fabric amounts given for the clothes are on the generous side. In many cases such as trousers or skirts you will need the length of the fabric called for but may have fabric width left over. This is because the patterns must be laid out in the direction of the arrows. Fabric amounts for the smaller items are not always given, as small scraps of material would be sufficient. Use your own judgement on trims, ribbons and laces.

Measuring for a good fit

The basic patterns fit dolls: 35–40cm (14–16in), 43–48cm (17–19in), 51–56cm (20–22in) and 58–63cm (23–25in).
There is no such thing as an average doll. They are all unique and can vary dramatically in their basic body measurements. It is very important that you take your all of your doll's measurements, compare them to the pattern and make any necessary adjustments before cutting out.

The seam allowance is already included in the patterns. Measure your doll against the pattern measurements and if your doll's measurements differ, adapt the pattern accordingly. Remember to add or subtract a 6mm (¼in) seam allowance to the pattern.

The basic measurements are:
 1 Chest width from under arms across chest.
 2 Back width from under arms across back.
 3 Waist circumference.
 4 Waist length from cervical point at base of neck to natural waistline.
 5 Hips circumference at widest point.
 6 Shoulder width from neck to arm joint.
 7 Sleeve length from arm joint at top of shoulder to wrist (or wherever you want the sleeve to end). Arm should be down.
 8 Wrist circumference. If the fingers are spread, make allowances so that the sleeve will go over the hand.
 9 Leg length from waist to hemline and from crotch to hemline.
10 Head circumference.

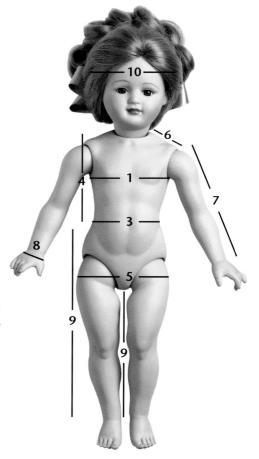

Adapting patterns

Trace the pattern pieces and adjust them according to your doll's measurements. Then trace the adjusted patterns on to lightweight card, transferring all the markings, and cut out. Lay the card pattern piece on the wrong side of the fabric and draw around it lightly with a ballpoint pen.

Try the garment on the doll several times during sewing. A 6mm (¼in) error can make a big difference when working on a small scale.

To ensure a good fit when adjusting patterns to fit a larger doll, take your doll's basic measurements and, using tissue paper, add the measurements to the original pattern pieces by cutting where indicated, inserting tissue paper taped in place and redrawing the outline. When you have adjusted all the pattern pieces use them to cut out a mock-up garment from cotton fabric, (curtain lining fabric works well and is inexpensive). Tack it together, don't use pins as they can stick to a cloth body and may scratch composition or porcelain bodies. Then try it on your doll, inside out, and make any other necessary adjustments before you cut the pattern out for real. When adjusting patterns to fit a smaller doll, use the guidelines as before but this time overlap the pieces before redrawing the outline. The diagrams below show basic adjustments to the main pattern pieces used in this book and where you should alter them. The patterns can be made larger by cutting where shown, inserting and taping in place tissue paper, shown as shaded areas in the diagrams below. The patterns can be made smaller by cutting where shown and overlapping the pattern pieces before redrawing the outlines where necessary.

Making basic adjustments

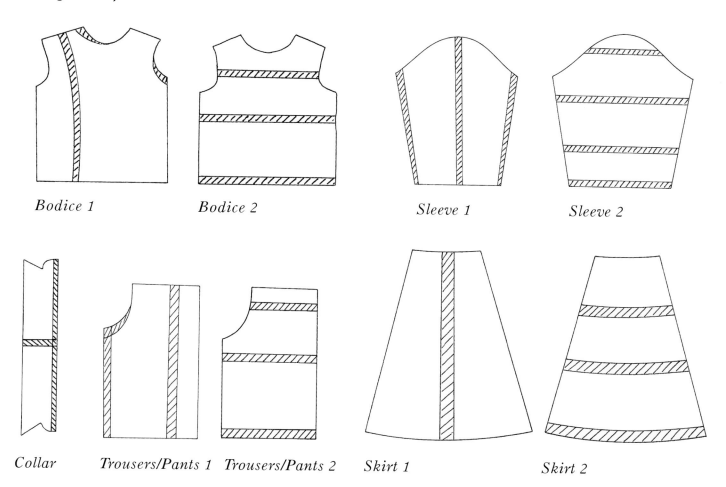

Bodice 1   *Bodice 2*   *Sleeve 1*   *Sleeve 2*

Collar   *Trousers/Pants 1*   *Trousers/Pants 2*   *Skirt 1*   *Skirt 2*

Tools and equipment

Along with basic sewing items
such as needles, tape measure,
fabric shears and a sewing machine,
a list of useful items for making
up the outfits, as well as the shoes
and hats, includes:

1 Tracing and tissue paper
2 Lightweight cardboard for
  shoe soles
3 Straight edge ruler
4 Scissors for cutting card
5 Small sharp scissors
6 Bodkin or safety pin for
  threading elastic through casings

7 Fabric glue
8 Clothes pegs for holding shoes
  and soles together while gluing
9 Awl for punching tiny holes
10 Gauge ruler to measure button
  placements and hems

A sleeve board for pressing tiny doll
sleeves is also useful

Basic techniques and stitches

 he following instructions include basic stitches and dressmaking techniques that are referred to in the making up of the patterns in this book. Read them carefully and refer back to them as directed.

Sewing techniques

Blind stitch is the preferred stitch when sewing small clothes and stitching hemlines. It is a neat and tidy stitch that is hardly seen and will not pull out. The needle travels under the folded edge of fabric coming up every 3–6mm (⅛–¼in) to pick up a tiny stitch on the surface before going back under the folded edge. Fig 1.

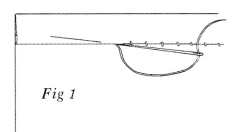

Fig 1

Overcasting is used if your machine does not have a zigzag stitch as an alternative to finishing a seam edge on fabrics that fray easily. Make sure the edges of the fabric are trimmed of any fraying threads before overcasting. Fig 2.

Buttonhole stitch is used if you prefer to work a buttonhole by hand. It is worked very close together. Set the

Fig 2

size and position of the buttonhole, allowing for the thickness of the thread, and mark with a faint pencil line. Using a single thread, run a line of small stitches around the mark, 3mm (⅛in) from the pencil line. Fig 3. With small sharp scissors slash along the pencil mark, knot the end of the thread and insert needle from front to back 12mm (½in) above the end of the hole. Bring the needle through the slash to the front. To work small uniform buttonhole stitches, from the slash to the tacking line, insert the needle back between the slash, coming out at the lower edge of the tacking. Loop the thread from left to right, under the point of the needle and pull the needle up so that the loop forms directly on the slash. Fig 4. Complete the buttonhole, fasten the thread at the back and trim off the original knot.

Fig 3

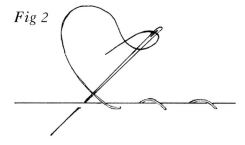

Fig 4

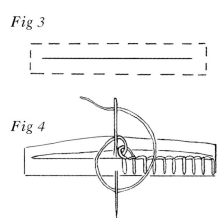

Run and fell seam is used for strength or to neaten fine fabrics that fray easily. With wrong sides together, run a 6mm (¼in) seam. Trim one seam allowance to 3mm (⅛in). Fig 5. Turn the untrimmed allowance over, encasing the trimmed edge, and stitch in place. Fig 6.

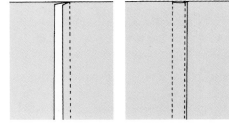

Fig 5   *Fig 6*

Snap fasteners are used where buttons would prove too bulky or where the area to be fastened is too small for a buttonhole to be worked. Using double thread, stitch through each hole of the snap three times making sure the stitches do not show on the right side. Tiny buttons may be sewn on the face side of the garment, over the snaps, to give the illusion of a button closure.

Flat elastic is used for stretch waistbands. Turn down 6mm (¼in) at the top of the waistline and press. Then turn down a further amount, wide enough so the elastic will slip easily through, and stitch in place leaving a small gap at the back seam to insert the elastic. Cut a length of elastic 12mm (½in) smaller than the doll's waist measurement and using a safety pin or bodkin attached to one end, guide it through the casing. When the end of the elastic is about to disappear, secure it with a pin and continue to pull the elastic through. When it comes full circle, fasten the ends together. Fig 7. Stitch the opening closed.

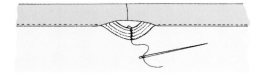

Fig 7

Shirring elastic is used when you want very narrow elastic as at the wrists or legs. Wrap the elastic snugly but not tightly around the part of the doll where you wish the elastic to go. Mark the elastic and cut it 5cm (2in) from the mark. This gives enough length to pull the elastic up to the mark and secure it. Lightly draw a pencil line on the wrong side of the fabric where the

elastic is to be sewn. Secure the end of the elastic with a few stitches at the start of the line and, using a zigzag stitch, encase it in the zigzags, pulling up the elastic as you sew. When you reach the end, secure the elastic at the mark and cut off the extra. If you do not have a zigzag stitch, use a doubled thread to make a casing by hand and weave the elastic through. Fig 8. Narrow 6mm (¼in) flat elastic is sewn on in a similar way only the zigzag stitch is sewn directly on top of the elastic as it is being pulled. Use a small stitch that will fit well inside the width of the elastic.

Fig 8

Interfacing gives body and maintains the shape of the fabric pattern piece. Iron-on interfacing comes in different weights. Light to medium weight is recommended for waistbands, cuffs, facings, collars and anything that needs a small amount of body. Medium to heavyweight is used for hats and shoes. When fusing interfacing to fabric, gently steam press rather than ironing back and forth as this can stretch the fabric, especially when fusing to a bias cut piece such as a collar or a hat brim. Interfacing is pressed on to the wrong side of the fabric. When a seam has been sewn, pull the interfacing away from the sewn edge and trim down to the line of stitching. This eliminates bulk when pressing the seam open.

Dressmaking techniques

Collars are made up separately and then sewn to the garment. The collar is always interfaced on one side. Use lightweight interfacing and press on to the wrong side of the fabric. With right sides facing, stitch around collar pieces leaving the neck edge open. Trim, turn and press. With right sides facing, pin and tack the collar as a whole to the bodice neckline centring the back and matching any markings. Pin the lining over the collar and stitch all around the neck edge. When the collar is completed the interfaced side should be on the top.

Sleeves can be made up by two different methods depending on the garment. With Method 1, a completed sleeve is set into a finished bodice. For Method 2, a sleeve is set into the bodice before the sleeve and side seams are sewn. Measure the length from the doll's armpit and add the hem and seam allowance before cutting. When adding trim such as rickrack or ribbon, stitch it on before the sleeve seam is stitched unless otherwise stated. Set the sleeve using one of the two methods described below and then turn up and stitch the hem if there is no cuff.

Method 1
- With right sides facing, align sleeve to armhole, tack or pin in place, distributing any gathers evenly.
- Stitch between the rows of gathering and then pull out the lower row of gathering stitches.
- Trim the edges on fabrics that fray and neaten by overcasting.

Method 2

- With right sides facing, align sleeve to armhole, tack or pin in place, distributing any gathers evenly.
- Stitch between the rows of gathering and then pull out the lower row of gathering stitches.
- With right sides facing, stitch up the sleeve continuing down the bodice side seam.

Bound sleeve openings are worked in sleeves which have buttoned cuffs. Cut a slit in the sleeve end where indicated on the pattern. Cut a strip of self-fabric on the bias, slightly longer than twice the length of the slit and 12mm (½in) wide. Press under 3mm (⅛in) on one side of the strip, spread the slit out horizontally and with right sides facing, pin the un-pressed edge of the strip to the edge of the slit. Stitch in place, pivoting the needle at the point. Take care not to stitch in any of the fullness of the sleeve. Fold the pressed edge of the strip over the raw edge and hand tack in place. Fig 9. Run gathering stitches (see Perfect gathers, right) around the sleeve opening. Fig 10. Pull up gathers and set in cuff.

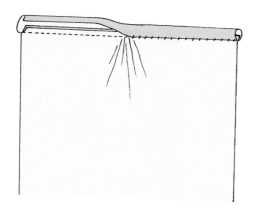

Fig 9

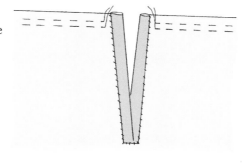

Fig 10

Buttoned cuffs are set into gathered sleeves with bound sleeve openings. Cuffs are interfaced on one side of the length using lightweight iron-on interfacing, which is pressed to the wrong side of the top half of the cuff. With right sides facing, fold the cuff in half lengthwise and stitch across each end. Pin right side of non-interfaced cuff to wrong side of sleeve end, pulling up gathers evenly and leaving an overlap at one end. Stitch in place. Turn the cuff over the sleeve end, turn in the raw edge and topstitch in place. Work a buttonhole and sew on button.

Dirndl skirt is a full skirt cut from a width of fabric three to four times the size of the doll's waist, depending upon the weight of the fabric and the desired fullness. The length is measured from the waist, adding seam and hem allowances. With right sides facing, stitch the skirt together at the back leaving a 5–7.5cm (2–3in) opening at the top. Work gathering stitches around the top edge of the skirt (see Perfect gathers, right). Pull up the gathers, distributing them evenly, and with right sides facing, pin skirt to bodice waistline matching centre of bodice to centre of skirt. Adjust the gathers and stitch between the rows.

Remove bottom row of gathers, press seam up. Finish according to the pattern instructions.

Perfect gathers are made using the longest stitch on your machine to run two parallel rows of stitching about 6mm (¼in) apart. Secure the threads at the start and then wrap the two other ends around your finger and pull up, distributing the gathers evenly. With right sides facing and the gathering stitches facing you, insert pins at right angles to the straight edge they are being joined to and adjust the gathers. Wind the ends of the threads over the end pins to secure and stitch between the two rows. Fig 11.

Fig 11

Waistbands are cut to twice the desired width plus seam allowance by the doll's waist measurement plus 2.5cm (1in). Iron lightweight interfacing to half the width of the waistband along one side of the length. With right sides facing, fold the waistband in half lengthwise and stitch across each end. Trim and turn to right side. Lay the non-interfaced side of the waistband against the wrong side of the skirt waist edge and pin and stitch in place. The left side of the waistband is flush with the left side of the skirt, and the extra 6mm (¼in) extends beyond the right side of the skirt to form an overlap. Turn and press 6mm (¼in) along the raw edge of the waistband then turn it over the skirt edge and topstitch in place. Make closures to fasten.

Socks and stockings are made from stretch cotton, T-shirt fabric, lace tights or from children's socks using the top edge as the top of the doll's socks. If using children's socks, cut the foot end off and cut the tube in half lengthwise so you have two pieces. Measure fabric snugly around doll's leg and using a short stitch on your machine, stitch rounding off one corner. Fig 12. Trim close to the seam and turn right side out.

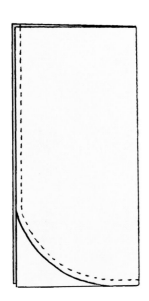

Fig 12

Shoes are made from fabric or leather. If the material is quite flimsy or stretches like glove leather, back the whole shoe with medium or heavyweight interfacing before cutting out. If the shoes or boots have buttons and the leather does not need to be interfaced, just iron interfacing where the buttons will go before cutting out the pattern piece. Do not press too hard and do not use steam on leather as it will stretch. To make a shoe that fits your doll's foot match the sole to the pattern and make adjustments. Remember to reverse pieces as instructed when cutting out so you do not end up with two left feet. Shoelace holes are made using an awl before the pieces of the shoe are stitched together.

The basic shoe
- Run a line of stay stitching 6mm (¼in) in around the lower edge of the uppers before stitching backs together unless otherwise instructed. Cut notches fairly close together in curved areas below the stay stitching. Fig 13.

Fig 13

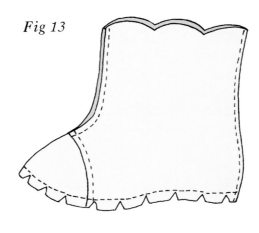

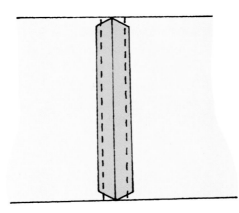

Fig 14

- Stitch the back of the shoe together, open out the seam, clip the corners off the top and bottom, and stitch seam open. Fig 14. Trim off excess.

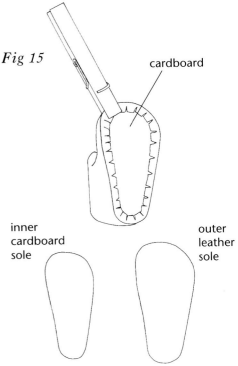

Fig 15

cardboard

inner cardboard sole

outer leather sole

- Insert cardboard sole, glue around notched edge of shoe upper and press to sole. Use the stay stitching as a guideline. It should be just under the sole. Mould the edges smoothly and clamp all around with clothes pegs. Fig 15. Wipe off excess glue with a damp cloth. The glue should set quickly so don't leave the pegs on the shoe too long as they can mark the leather.
- When the sole has dried, spread glue on the inner cardboard sole and press in place filling the area inside the notched edges. Use clothes pegs to hold it in place until completely dry.
- When the inner sole is fixed, spread glue over the bottom of the shoe and fix the leather sole. Make sure the edges are securely glued.

Helpful sewing hints

• For machine sewing a size 10 (70) or 11 (75) needle is good for cotton and silks and size 14 (90) for heavier fabrics like woollens and velveteen. A ballpoint needle prevents snagging when sewing silk. Use a small stitch when sewing dolls clothes. Change the needle when it becomes blunt and keep your machine well oiled and free from lint.

• When stitching material such as velvet or satin, sew slowly pulling gently on the fabric and place your pins at right angles to the stitching line to prevent the material from walking.

• For hand sewing a thin needle like a milliner or darner is easier to use than an ordinary sharp. They are longer and thinner and once you get used to them you will probably find a shorter needle quite awkward.

• Tissue paper placed under leather when sewing will help the fabric run much more smoothly on the sewing machine.

• When hemming or blind stitching use a single thread and close, neat stitches. Cotton or cotton-polyester mixed thread should match the garment colour as closely as possible. Use silk thread on silk fabrics – strands pulled from the fabric itself and used as thread make the stitches nearly invisible.

• If you are using a fabric that frays easily, finish raw edges that will remain raw by machine zigzag stitch, cutting with pinking shears or overcasting by hand before stitching together.

• Always cut ribbon on the bias. A tiny amount of fabric glue or 'Fray Check' will help to stop it from fraying.

• Thread the needle as it comes off the spool, knotting the end you cut off. This will prevent the thread snarling.

• Thread is expensive so if you have a lot of ruffles or gathering stitches to do, use a lesser quality thread as it will be removed in the end anyway. If you use quality thread for gathers, when it is pulled out be sure to save it for hand stitching.

• Dressmakers' pins are best on lightweight fabrics. They are a bit longer and thinner than ordinary pins, which makes working on heavier fabrics easier. Use silk pins when working with silk and taffeta. Pins can become blunt so if they start to catch the fabric replace them.

• Use a piece of muslin or an old tea towel as a pressing cloth to prevent damage when working with delicate or antique fabrics. When ironing woollens the pressing cloth should be slightly damp and the fabric ironed slowly so that the dampness is driven into the fabric below.

• When pressing velveteen, lay the fabric face down on to a clean fluffy towel to prevent crushing the pile, then gently steam press on the wrong side of the fabric.

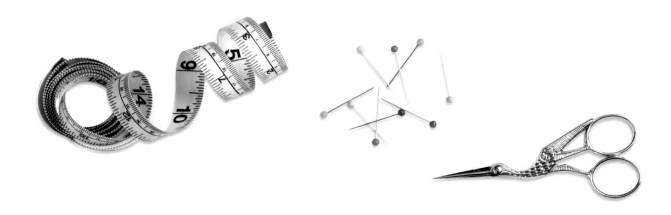

Alice in Wonderland

When Lewis Carroll wrote *Alice's Adventures in Wonderland* in 1865, it was an immediate success. Who could forget the fall down the White Rabbit's hole, the elusive Cheshire Cat, the preposterous tea party or the eccentric croquet game with the bad-tempered Queen of Hearts? The nonsensical characters in this strange and exciting world, as seen through a child's eyes, are an integral part of the book's charm, making it one of the best-loved classics of our time.

'Alice thought she had never seen such a curious croquet ground in her life: it was all ridges and furrows; the croquet balls were live hedgehogs, the mallets live flamingoes, and the soldiers had to double themselves up and stand on their hands and feet to make the arches.'

The doll shown is a Barnaby reproduction of a German doll from the author's collection. She is 48cm (19in) high.

Alice

'Oh, I've had such a curious dream!'

This outfit fits a 43–48cm (17–19in) doll.

you will need

¼ metre/yard white calico

¼ metre/yard Alice blue calico

1 metre/yard narrow red satin ribbon

3 buttons

1 shank button

25cm (10in) boning

2 shoe buttons

25cm (10in) square black leather

Shirring elastic

25cm (10in) of 5cm (2in) wide blue ribbon

Instructions

Dress

Alice's dress is a classic design made from blue calico. It has puffed sleeves, a Peter Pan collar and full dirndl skirt. The bodice is lined with self-fabric.

Pattern pieces required: Bodice front 1A, Bodice back 1B, Peter Pan collar 1C, Puffed sleeve 1D.
Cutting list: From blue calico cut two 1A, four 1B (two reversed), four 1C, two 1D and one dirndl skirt three times the doll's waist measurement by 20cm (8in) long.
Before cutting out collar, iron lightweight interfacing to the wrong side of the fabric for two collar pieces.

Making up
- With right sides facing, stitch bodice front and backs together at shoulders. Press seams open. Repeat for lining.
- With right sides facing, stitch the interfaced collar pieces to the non-interfaced pieces around the

curved edge, leaving the neck edge open. Trim, turn and press. When the collar is finished the interfaced sides should be on the top.

- With right sides facing, centre and pin the collar pieces to the bodice neckline. Stitch in place.
- With right sides facing, pin the lining over the bodice, sandwiching the collar. Stitch up one side, around the neckline and down the other side. Trim corners, notch neckline, turn and press. From this point the bodice and lining are worked as one piece.
- Stitch the lining to the bodice at the side fronts, around the sleeve openings and down the side backs to keep them together.
- Turn a 6mm (¼in) hem at the bottom of the sleeves. Set shirring elastic 12mm (½in) above the hem (see page 10).
- Run gathering stitches at the top of the sleeves and set using Method 2 (see page 11).
- With right sides facing, fold skirt and stitch together leaving 4cm (1½in) open at the top. Press seam open. Turn up 6mm (¼in) at the bottom and press. Run two rows of gathering stitches at the top and pull up gathers.
- With right sides facing, pin skirt to bodice adjusting the gathers, and stitch in place. Press up seam allowance and topstitch to hold.
- Turn up a further 2.5cm (1in) at the bottom of skirt and hand hem.
- Work buttonhole closures at the back where indicated.

Apron

The pinafore-style apron has large ruffles at the sleeves. The bib buttons down the back and the sash waistband ties in a big bow.

Pattern pieces required: Bib front 1E, Bib back 1F, Sleeve ruffle 1G, Apron pocket 1H.

Cutting list: From white calico cut two 1E, four 1F (two reversed), four 1G, two 1H, one skirt 28cm (11in) wide by 15cm (6in) long, two waistbands 4cm (1½in) wide by 23cm (9in) long and two ties 6cm (2½in) wide by 38cm (15in) long.

Making up

- Turn down 6mm (¼in) at the top of the pocket and stitch. With right sides facing, turn top of pocket over 12mm (½in) and stitch together at sides. Clip corners. Run a single line of gathering stitches around pocket from the turn down. Fig 1. Turn pocket to the right side and press.

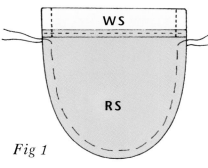

Fig 1

- Using red thread, stitch ribbon trim across top of pocket, turning in the ends. Gently pull up the gathering stitches, turning the edges in smoothly and press in place. Repeat for second pocket.
- Turn a 6mm (¼in) hem down sides and across bottom of apron. Using red thread, stitch ribbon trim over the hemstitching.
- Place pockets 4cm (1½in) from the side edges and 4.5cm (1¾in) from the bottom of skirt and topstitch in place.

- Stitch bib front to backs at the shoulders. Press seams open. Repeat for lining.
- Stitch sleeve ruffles together around curved edge. Turn, press and stitch on ribbon trim.
- Run two rows of gathering stitches along the raw edges of ruffles and pin to bib front and back across shoulders between indication marks. Place most of the gathers at the top and stitch in place. Remove gathering stitches.
- With right sides facing, stitch bib lining to bib at neckline and down backs. Tuck in sleeve ruffles and stitch up all four sides about 12mm (½in) into ruffles.

Lewis Carroll was the pen name of Charles Dodgson, a mathematics tutor at Christ Church College, Oxford, England. 'Alice', one of Carroll's most famous creations, was based on a real little girl who was the daughter of the Dean of Christ Church College.

- With wrong sides facing, centre, pin and stitch the skirt to the lower edge of waistband lining and the bodice front and backs to the upper edge. Fig 2.
- To make the ties, stitch 3mm (⅛in) hem along both long edges. Turn up 6mm (¼in) at one end and fold one corner up to meet the opposite side. Tack in place. Fig 3.

- Gather the other ends of the ties and with wrong sides facing, secure a tie into each end of the waistband lining. Pin the waistband over the waistband lining and topstitch all around the waistband. Fig 4.
- Make a button loop closure at the top back (see box below right) and sew on a shank button.

This gives a finished edge to the sides and lets you turn the bodice right side out easily. Trim, clip curves, turn to right side and press. Hand tack the remaining openings closed.

- Press in 6mm (¼in) all the way around each waistband.
- Run two rows of gathering stitches along top of apron skirt and pull up to 9cm (3½in).

Alice Pleasance Liddell, the real 'Alice', and her sisters would accompany Charles Dodgson on picnics and boating trips down the River Thames on quiet, summer afternoons. It was on one of these excursions that Dodgson was inspired to write *Alice's Adventures Underground* which was later published, under his pseudonym Lewis Carroll, as *Alice's Adventures in Wonderland*.

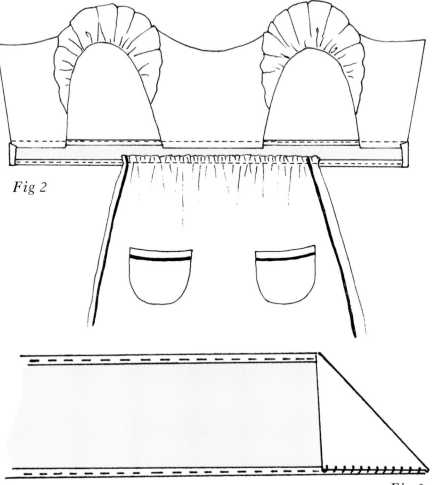

Fig 2

Fig 3

Fig 4

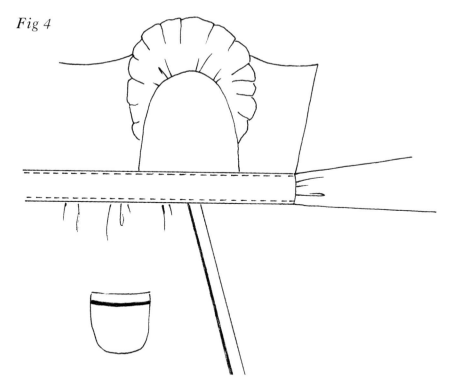

Mary Jane shoes

Alice's shoes are made from leather and have a buttoned strap.

Pattern pieces required: Upper 2C, Inner sole 2D, Outer sole 2E.
Cutting list: From leather cut two 2C, two 2E (one reversed) and two straps 6mm (¼in) wide to fit over doll's foot plus 12mm (½in). From cardboard cut two 2D.

Making up
- Stitch the strap inside the shoe where indicated.
- Round off the other end of strap and cut a slit for a small shank button or bead to fit through.
- Follow the basic shoe instructions (see page 12).
- Stitch the button/bead to the outside of shoe where indicated.

Button loops

Work several uniform loose stitches close together at the edge of the fabric where the loop will go. Pull the needle out at the base of the stitches and loop the thread from left to right, under the point of the needle before pulling the needle up. Push the stitches snugly together. Continue the stitches until the loop is completely covered. Fasten off the thread securely.

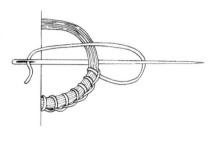

Alice band

Make a casing from ribbon or bias tape to fit over the doll's head coming just below the ears. Insert a piece of boning through the casing and secure the ends. Work button loops at each end and fasten the band to the hair through the loops with kirby grips (bobby pins).

collector's focus

In November 1928, the original handwritten manuscript of *Alice's Adventures Underground* went on sale at Sotheby's. Inscribed 'A Christmas gift to a dear child in memory of a summer day', it was bought for GB£15,400 which was then the highest price ever paid for a book at a British auction.

The doll shown is a reproduction of a French antique doll by Thuiller, c.1870–90 from the author's collection. She is 51cm (20in) high.

Alice's Adventures in Wonderland sold over a quarter of a million copies before the author's death in 1898. Today it is still a favourite of children around the world and has been translated into more than 60 languages.

The Queen of Hearts

'Off with his head!'

This outfit fits a 51–56cm (20–22in) doll.

you will need

1 metre/yard red satin backed crêpe

½ metre/yard pink satin

½ metre/yard white organza

Selection of ribbons, lace-edged trims and braid trims

Heart-shaped beads in various sizes

Pearl beads

2½ metres/yards flexi-lace or seam binding

Lightweight iron-on interfacing

A small amount of polyester filling

Some elaborate lace or 15cm (6in) circumference lace doily for the Vandyke collar

Shirring elastic

3 buttons

Fabric stiffener

Glue

Piece of gold art board

Wooden chopstick

Gold paint

25cm (10in) square red leather

61cm (24in) of 12mm (½in) wide red satin ribbon

Instructions

Gown

The square-necked bodice buttons down the back and is embellished with heart-shaped beads across the neck. It is interfaced and lined with self-fabric.

The long sleeves have a wrist ruffle and are puffed in three different sections. The pink bodice is attached to a red dirndl skirt with a long train. The train's fullness is achieved by tight gathers.

Pattern pieces required: Bodice front 1I, Bodice back 1J, Royal sleeve 1K, Skirt front 1L, Skirt back 1M.
Cutting list: From red satin backed crêpe cut one 1L, and one 1M. From pink satin cut two 1I and four 1J (two reversed). From white organza cut two 1K.

Making up
- Iron interfacing to the bodice before cutting out.
- With right sides facing, stitch bodice front and backs at shoulders, press seams open. Repeat for lining.
- With right sides facing and lace trim sandwiched at neckline, stitch bodice to lining around neckline and down backs. Trim, turn and press.
- Fold sleeve where indicated and overcast sides and top. Run stitching where indicated to create three casings. Using a bodkin, insert lengths of shirring elastic into the casings and secure at one end. The other ends of the elastic should protrude slightly.
- Run gathering stitches at tops of sleeves and set sleeves using Method 2 (see page 11).
- Measure doll's arm at wrist, below elbow and at shoulder and pull elastics up accordingly and secure. Fold sleeve in half and stitch seam, catching elastic ends, then continuing down side of bodice. Repeat for other sleeve and side.

- Run a zigzag stitch along lower edge of bodice, and top and side raw edges of skirt.
- With right sides facing, stitch skirt front to back. Press seams open.
- To make a faced opening at centre back cut a small rectangle of fabric 10cm (4in) by 5cm (2in) and hem three sides. With right sides facing, place rectangle at centre back over intended opening and run two lines of stitching about 8cm (3in) long each side of opening and 3mm (⅛in) apart, tapering to nothing. Cut between the stitching. Fig 1. Turn the rectangle through the opening, overlapping one edge over the other, press and hand stitch in place using small stitches. Fig 2.

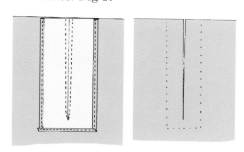

Fig 1   *Fig 2*

- Stitch flexi-lace or seam binding to bottom of skirt, notch curved edge of skirt. Fig 3. Turn hem up and hand stitch. Fig 4.

Fig 3

Fig 4

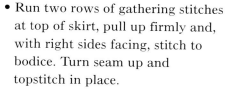

- Run two rows of gathering stitches at top of skirt, pull up firmly and, with right sides facing, stitch to bodice. Turn seam up and topstitch in place.
- Make buttonhole closures at the back where indicated.
- Stitch decorative hearts to front of bodice as shown.

Tablier

The tablier ties around the doll's waist over the gown and under the jacket, hanging down the front. It is elaborately decorated with lace, ribbon, braid and heart motifs, which are slightly padded to make them stand out.

Cutting list: From pink satin cut two tabliers the length of the skirt from the bodice by 7.5cm (3in) across the top edge widening to 13cm (5in) at the bottom edge. From red satin backed crêpe cut three heart motifs in varying sizes.

Making up

- Iron interfacing to one side of the tablier. This will be the front.
- Decorate the front tablier with lace and ribbon and sew on heart motifs (see box above right).
- With right sides facing, stitch front tablier to back down sides and across bottom sandwiching lace trim at the bottom. (Note: Be careful not to catch the lace when stitching up the sides of the tablier because it will not turn down.) Trim, turn to right side, press and overcast the top of tablier.
- Hand stitch braid around the side and bottom edges of the tablier.
- Cut about 61cm (24in) of 12mm (½in) red satin ribbon and bind the top edge leaving ends free to tie around the doll's waist.

Jacket

The jacket is made from the same red satin backed crêpe lined with pink satin. It fastens at the waistline revealing the decorated bodice of the gown. A gathered basque finishes the bottom edge and two pink hearts are sewn to the fronts. The shoulder wings are trimmed with braid and a Vandyke collar accents the neckline.

Pattern pieces required: Jacket front 1N, Jacket back 1P, Jacket basque 1Q, Shoulder wing 1R.
Cutting list: From red satin backed crêpe cut two 1N (one reversed), one 1P and one 1Q.
From pink satin cut two 1N (one reversed), one 1P, one 1Q and two 1R.

Making up

- With right sides facing, stitch jacket fronts to jacket back at shoulders and down sides. Press seams open. Repeat for lining.
- With right sides facing, stitch jacket to lining around sleeves and down the front leaving neckline open to the indication marks. Trim

Heart motifs

The heart motifs are made from red satin backed with iron-on interfacing. Read making up instructions before cutting out.

Making up

- Use a pencil to transfer the heart motifs (see page 81), to the interfaced side of the satin.
- Run a line of stitching on the pencil line of the heart shapes and cut out motifs 6mm (¼in) outside the stitching line. Notch as shown. Fig 5.
- Turn edges into the heart using the stitching as a guideline and hand stitch in place. Be careful not to let the stitching show on the front. Press motifs.

- Lay a heart in place on the tablier. Start at one side and hand stitch most of the way around. When you are 12mm (½in) from the start, push a small amount of polyester filling into the heart. An orangewood stick works well. Gently push the filling into the corners and around the edges but don't make the hearts too hard, leave them soft. Stitch opening closed.

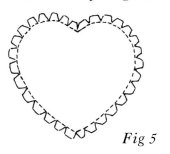

Fig 5

and turn to right side. Turn in the raw edges of the bodice and lining at the neckline and press. Overcast jacket and lining together along the bottom edge and press.
- With right sides facing, stitch basque and lining together leaving the top edge open. Trim, turn and zigzag stitch along the top edge.
- Gather top edge of basque and attach to bottom edge of jacket, matching notches with side seams.
- Turn the seam up into the jacket, press and topstitch in place. (Note: Stitch the seam down at the very front edges so they don't poke out.)
- With right sides facing, fold one shoulder wing in half lengthwise and stitch together leaving an opening at centre for turning. Turn. Repeat for second wing.
- Stuff shoulder wings with filling, firmly but not hard, and stitch openings closed.

- Wrap decorative braid around shoulder wings in a spiral, stitching in place as you wrap.
- Attach the wings to the outside of shoulders matching dots.
- Work a hook and eye closure at the waistline front.

Vandyke collar

Use a lacy doily at least 15cm (6in) in circumference for the collar.

Making up

- Carefully cut the doily up to the centre following the shape of the design. Cut the centre out of the doily so you can open it out and fit it around the doll's neck with the front of the collar matching the indication marks on the jacket. The back of the collar should be about 5cm (2in) high. Taper the doily to 3cm (1¼in) at the fronts and trim off excess.
- Insert collar between bodice and lining, and topstitch in place.
- Holding the jacket with the collar over waxed paper or kitchen

towel, brush fabric stiffener on to the collar being careful not to get it on the jacket. Use a hairdryer to accelerate drying. When nearly dry, put the jacket on the doll, making sure the hair is out of the way, and shape the collar with your hands. Cotton wool placed under the collar will help hold it in place until completely dry.

Coronet

The coronet consists of a satin circlet with decorative trim beneath a crown of hearts and pearls. The crown is held in place by the circlet, which sits on top of the doll's head.

Pattern pieces required: Crown 1S.
Cutting list: From pink satin cut a rectangle 9cm (3½in) wide by 33cm (13in) long.
From gold card cut one 1S.

Making up

- Press the raw edges of the rectangle in 6mm (¼in) at the short ends. With right sides facing, stitch the long edges together. Turn to the right side.
- Stuff the circlet firmly, but not too hard, with the filling.
- Wrap decorative trim around the circlet in a spiral, as for the shoulder wings, and stitch in place tucking in ends.
- Match the ends of the circlet and hand stitch to form a circle.
- Glue hearts to the three points and pearl beads to the hearts and around the top edge of the crown.

Sceptre

The sceptre is made from a gold chopstick with a padded heart motif glued on to the end.

Making up

- Paint the chopstick gold and let the paint dry completely.
- Back the red satin with interfacing before cutting out two large heart motifs.
- With right sides facing, stitch the motifs together leaving a 12mm (½in) opening at the bottom point for turning and stuffing.
- Trim to opening. Press edges back at opening and turn to right side. You should have a neat point at the bottom where it's pressed.
- Stuff polyester filling into the heart shape until it is quite firm.
- Work the pointed end of the chopstick up into the centre of the heart making sure it is surrounded by filling. Secure the heart to the chopstick with a spot of glue at the open end. Stitch pearl beads around the edge of the heart. The decorative ornament is optional.

Slippers

The Queen's leather slippers have heart-shaped uppers and are embellished with tiny heart beads.

Pattern pieces required: Upper 2F, Inner sole 2G, Outer sole 2H.
Cutting list: From leather cut two 2F and two 2H (one reversed). From cardboard cut two 2G.

Making up

- Follow basic shoe instructions (see page 12).
- Stitch tiny heart-shaped or pearl beads where indicated.

23

What's underneath?

Alice's underwear consists of a camisole, drawers and a full petticoat. The Queen of Hearts wears a camisole, pantalets, half-petticoat and a bustle.

you will need

About ¾ metre/yard of white cotton lawn or batiste

Small piece of scalloped edge lace fabric

Assorted lace trimmings

Eyelet lace and red ribbon for insertion

Narrow flat elastic

Small amount of polyester filling

3 buttons

2 snap fasteners

Instructions

Alice's camisole

The camisole has two pintucks and a row of lace on either side of the buttoned front. It is self-lined.

Pattern pieces required: Camisole front 1W, Camisole back 1X, Camisole front lining 1Y.
Cutting list: From cotton lawn cut two 1W (one reversed), two 1X and two 1Y (one reversed).

Making up
• Stitch lace trim to bodice fronts as indicated. Fold first pintuck on solid guideline, steam press and stitch along the broken guideline. Work second tuck in the same way. Press tucks towards the lace trim.

did you know?
Alice Pleasance Liddell, the real 'Alice', had short brown hair with a fringe and was a talented girl in her own right. She was a gifted artist and watercolourist, prolific in writing letters, journals and diaries. Alice died on 16 November 1934 at the age of 82.

- With right sides facing, stitch fronts and back together at shoulders. Press seams open. Repeat for lining.
- With right sides facing, stitch bodice to lining around the sleeve openings and all around the outside leaving an opening where indicated, for turning. Trim curves, clip corners and turn through to right side and press.
- With right sides facing, stitch bodice and lining together at sides and across bottom fronts leaving an opening at the back for turning. Clip corners, turn, press and hand stitch opening closed.
- Work buttonholes and sew on buttons where indicated.

Alice's drawers

The drawers have an elasticized waistline and are quite plain with a lace trim at the legs.

Pattern pieces required: Drawers 1V.
Cutting list: From cotton lawn cut two 1V (one reversed).

Making up
- Stitch a 6mm (¼in) hem at the bottom of each leg. Stitch lace trim over hem.
- With right sides facing, stitch fronts and backs together at crotch.

Clip curves and press seams open.
- Stitch up one leg and down the other. Press seam open.
- Work an elasticized waistline using flat elastic (see page 10).

Alice's petticoat

The petticoat buttons at the back, has a self-lined bodice and a lace and ribbon trim at the hemline.

Pattern pieces required: Bodice front 1T, Bodice back 1U.
Cutting list: From cotton lawn cut two 1T, four 1U (two reversed) and one skirt approximately 15cm (6in) long by 66cm (26in) wide.

Making up
- With right sides facing, stitch bodice front to bodice backs at shoulders. Press seams open. Repeat for lining.
- With right sides of bodice and lining facing, stitch around neck opening, down the backs and around armholes. Trim.
- With right sides of bodice and lining facing, stitch sides together. Press seams open, turn bodice over lining and press again.
- With right sides facing, fold the skirt and stitch together leaving a 4cm (1½in) opening at top. Press seam open.
- Run two rows of gathering stitches across the top of skirt and pull up.
- Stitch right side of lining only to wrong side of skirt, adjusting gathers. Turn bodice down over skirt, turn up raw edges and topstitch in place.
- Turn up a 6mm (¼in) hem and add lace and ribbon trim.
- Work buttonhole closures where indicated (see page 9).

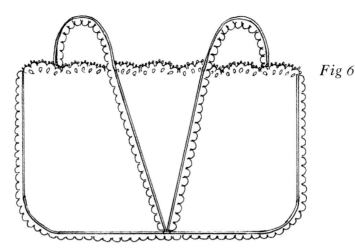

Fig 6

Queen's camisole

The camisole is made from one piece of scalloped lace with narrow lace trim decorating the front and forming the straps. It fastens at the back with two snap fasteners.

Pattern piece required: Camisole 2A.
Cutting list: From lace fabric cut one 2A with the scalloped edge at the top. If the lace has a symmetrical design, centre it at the fold.

Making up

- Hand stitch lace trim from centre bottom to indication mark A. Leave about 11.5cm (4¼in) for the strap and pin the other end to the wrong side of indication mark B. Fig 6. Try the camisole on the doll, adjust straps and stitch in place.
- Starting at the top, stitch lace trim down the right side, around the bottom edge and up the left side, turning in the ends.

- Press very narrow strips of iron-on interfacing to the inside side edges for reinforcement. The strips should be narrow enough so that they don't show through to the front of the camisole.
- Sew two snap fasteners at the back where indicated.

Queen's pantalets

The pantalets are long drawers with lace and trim at the ankles.

Pattern piece required: Pantalet 1Z.
Cutting list: From cotton lawn cut two 1Z (one reversed).

Making up

- Work as for Alice's drawers (see page 25).

Queen's bustle

The polyester-filled bustle sits over the petticoat and under the skirt. It ties at the front.

Pattern pieces required: Bustle 2B.
Cutting list: From cotton lawn cut two 2B.

Making up

- Transfer and stitch darts on both pattern pieces. Backstitch at the widest part and taper off the tip without backstitching.
- With right sides facing, stitch across the top of the bustle.

- Pin narrow ribbon ties at the top of each side with the ties tucked inside the bustle. Stitch around the bustle leaving opening for turning and stuffing.
- Turn bustle to right side (the ties will now be on the right side) and stuff with the polyester filling. Stuff firmly, not tightly, getting the filling into the corners using an orangewood stick or similar.
- Hand stitch the opening closed.

Queen's half-petticoat

The petticoat has three rows of pintucks, eyelet lace threaded with ribbon and a ruffle at the bottom. It is worked as a dirndl skirt with a waistband (see page 11).

Cutting list: From cotton lawn cut a skirt 112cm (44in) wide by 30.5cm (12in) long, a waistband 5cm (2in) wide by the doll's waistline plus 2cm (1in) and a ruffle 4cm (1½in) deep by twice the width of the skirt.

Making up
- Work three 6mm (¼in) pintucks, 2cm (1in) from the bottom of the skirt (see page 24).
- Work a 6mm (¼in) hem on one length of the ruffle and run gathering stitches along the other edge. With right sides facing, pin and stitch ruffle to the edge of the skirt, adjusting the gathering to fit.
- Stitch eyelet lace between the pintucks and the ruffle. Using a safety pin, thread red ribbon through the eyelets.
- Fold the skirt, right sides facing, and stitch seam from the bottom up, over the ruffle, lace and pintucks, leaving 5cm (2in) open at the top. Press seam open.

- Run two rows of gathering stitches at the top of the skirt and pull up.
- With right sides facing, fold waistband in half lengthwise and stitch ends. Turn and press.
- Pin right side of waistband to wrong side of skirt leaving a 2cm

(¾in) allowance on the left side for overlapping the waistband. Adjust the gathers evenly and stitch in place. Turn the waistband over the skirt and topstitch in place.
- Work a buttonhole on overlap and sew on button.

The Wizard of Oz

Frank L Baum's American fairytale, *The Wonderful Wizard of Oz* tells the story of Dorothy, who is carried off by a cyclone to the land of Oz where she is aided by Glinda, the Good Witch of the North. She sets off with the most unlikely travelling companions, a scarecrow, tin man and a lion, to find the Emerald City and the Wizard who is said to be able to make all wishes come true.

'If I ever go looking for my hearts desire again,
I won't look any further than my own
backyard; because if it isn't there, I never
really lost it to begin with.'

The doll shown is a modern German doll from the author's collection. She is 40cm (16in) high.

did you know?

Frank Lyman Baum was born in 1856 in New York State. Due to a heart defect he spent his childhood reading instead of playing. He had a variety of jobs including actor, playwright, salesman and journalist. He also bred chickens, owned a newspaper and opened a store called Baum's Bazaar. Frank loved children and had a gift for storytelling. Children often stopped him in the street demanding stories.

Dorothy

'This doesn't look like Kansas to me!'

This outfit fits a 35–40cm (14–16in) doll.

you will need

¼ metre/yard blue cotton gingham

30cm (12in) white cotton calico

Narrow blue rickrack braid

3 buttons

2 shank buttons

Red glitter glue (available from craft and haberdashery shops)

Narrow red ribbon

Instructions

Dress

Dorothy's blue gingham frock has the look of a pinafore over a white blouse but in fact it is made in one piece. The neck of the bodice is gathered into a rouleau collar, which is trimmed with blue rickrack as are the sleeves. The dress buttons down the back and has a full dirndl skirt.

Pattern pieces required: Bodice upper front 3J, Bodice lower front 3K, Bodice upper back 3L, Bodice lower back 3M, Bodice front lining 3N, Bodice back lining 3P and Sleeve 3Q.
Cutting list: From gingham cut one 3K, two 3M (one reversed), four 2.5cm (1in) strips of fabric; two measured twice around the body and two measured over the shoulders from waist front to waist back. Cut one dirndl skirt three times the doll's waist measurement by 18cm (7in).
From white calico cut one 3J, two 3L (one reversed), one 3N, two 3P (one reversed), two 3Q, one collar

3cm (1¼in) wide by 15cm (6in) long and two cuffs 3cm (1¼in) wide by 11.5cm (4½in) long.

Making up

- Gather lower edge of bodice upper front. With right sides facing, stitch to bodice lower front matching notches. Press seam down.
- With right sides facing, stitch bodice upper and lower backs together matching notches. Press seam down.
- Stitch bodice front and backs together at shoulders. Repeat for lining. Press seams open.
- With right sides facing, fold collar in half lengthwise and stitch across each end. Trim, turn and press.
- Gather neck edge of bodice upper front between notches. With collar sandwiched between bodice and lining, stitch around neckline and down backs.
- Iron interfacing to the wrong side of cuff, on one half of the length. With right sides facing, stitch cuff to sleeve. Fig 1. Hand stitch rickrack to right side over seam line. Attach sleeve to bodice using Method 2 (see page 11). Turn cuff under sleeve, turn in 6mm (¼in) and hand stitch.

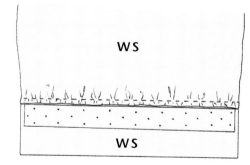

Fig 1

- Turn in and press top and bottom edges of the two short and two long decorative bodice strips to make 12mm (½in) wide strips. Pin the shorter strips at the waistline and at the top gingham edge of the bodice, turning the ends over the back opening. Tuck the longer strips under the top strip at the back then topstitch the shorter strips along both the top and bottom edges, catching in the straps. Turn the raw edge up at the front of the strap and secure them on the bottom strip with two shank buttons.
- Hand stitch rickrack at the seam line of the collar.
- Work buttonholes and stitch on three buttons at the back where indicated.

Ruby slippers

In the film Dorothy's ruby slippers grant her a wish when she clicks her heels together. These slippers are made from leather and red glitter glue adds the sparkle.

Pattern pieces required: Upper 4H, sole 4I, Inner sole 4J.

Cutting list: From red leather cut two 4H and two 4I (one reversed). From cardboard cut two 4J and two 4I.

Making up

- Follow the basic instructions to make up the shoes (see page 12).

- Tie two tiny bows made from narrow red ribbon and glue to the toes of the shoes. Paint the shoe uppers and bows with red glitter glue. Apply several coats letting the glue dry between each coat.

did you know?

In the original story Dorothy's ruby slippers were silver shoes. They were all that was left of the Wicked Witch of the East when Dorothy's house landed on top of her. The shoes would give her magic powers enabling her to go home – but only after she killed the Wicked Witch of the West.

The doll shown is Queen Louise, a reproduction of a German Armand Marseille doll. She is 51cm (20in) high.

Glinda – the Good Witch of the North

'Close your eyes, click your heels together three times and repeat, there's no place like home, there's no place like home.'

This outfit fits a 51–56cm (20–22in) doll.

you will need

¼ metre/yard pink acetate satin fabric

½ metre/yard star embossed white netting fabric

Small amount of pink velveteen for slippers

2 metres/2½ yards narrow silver rickrack

3 snap fasteners

Decorative flower or similar motif

Decorative shoe buckles

Lightweight card

Sheet of silver card

Silver glitter glue and paint

Glue or glue gun

Chopstick

Star-shaped sequins and tiny glass beads

Instructions

Gown

The gown's low cut bodice is self-lined and gathered in netting. It fastens at the back and the sleeves are folded double and billow out into delicate gossamer puffs. The whole gown shimmers with stars caught up in the netting that flows over a full dirndl skirt.

Pattern pieces required: Bodice front 4B, Bodice back 4C and Sleeve 4D.
Cutting list: From pink satin cut two 4B, four 4C (two reversed) and one dirndl skirt four times the doll's waist by the length plus seam and hem allowance.
From netting cut two 4C (one reversed), two 4D, one bodice piece about 20cm (8in) by 30.5cm (12in) and two skirt pieces as above (without hem allowance).

Making up

- Run a row of gathering stitches across the centre short width of the bodice piece of netting stopping 2.5cm (1in) from the lower edge.
- With both fabrics right side up, place the gathered rectangle over the bodice front and pin along the top and bottom edges. Pull the gathering stitches up, carefully spacing the gathers around the sleeve openings. Stitch the netting to the bodice down over the central gathering stitches.
- Stitch all around the bodice close to the edge and trim off the excess netting. Fig 1.
- With both right sides facing upwards, lay netting bodice backs over the bodice backs and stitch together, close to the edge, all the way around, as for bodice front.

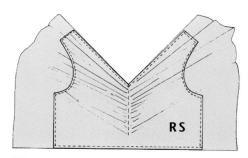

Fig 1

RS

- With right sides facing, stitch the bodice front to the bodice backs at the shoulders. Repeat for linings. Press seams open.
- With right sides facing, stitch the bodice and bodice lining together around the neckline. Trim, turn and press.
- With wrong sides facing, fold sleeves along the bottom edge. Overcast the top edges together and run two rows of gathering stitches. Set sleeves using Method 2 (see page 11). Trim sleeve seams close to the stitching. Press side seams open.
- Overcast the bottom of the bodice to hold bodice and lining together and to stop fraying.
- With right sides facing, stitch satin skirt together at the back leaving 7.5cm (3in) open at the top. Press seam open. Put the two netting skirts together and repeat stitching. Trim seam close to stitching. Turn the 7.5cm (3in) opening of the netting back and stitch 3mm ($\frac{1}{8}$in) in from the edge. Trim close to stitching.
- With right sides facing up, lay the netting skirt over the satin skirt matching openings and overcast the layers together at the top edge.
- Turn 6mm ($\frac{1}{4}$in) up at the bottom of the satin skirt.
- Run two rows of gathering stitches around the top of the three layers of skirt. With right sides facing, pin skirt to bodice adjusting the gathers evenly and stitch in place. Press seam allowance up and topstitch in place.
- Hand stitch rickrack trim to the waistline covering the topstitching and tucking in the ends at the back. Add decorative trim at the

centre of the bodice as shown and sew snap fasteners at the back where indicated.
- Hand hem satin skirt and stitch rickrack trim to bottom edge of each of the netting skirts.
- Stitch star sequins held by a glass bead to skirt, bodice and sleeves placing them at random.

did you know?

The Wonderful Wizard of Oz, first published in 1900, was so popular that Frank L Baum wrote 13 more Oz novels before his death in 1919. He did not intend to write so many sequels, but the requests from children were incessant. *Glinda of Oz* was the last book he wrote. It was published in 1920 after his death.

Crown

Glinda wears a tall silver crown decorated with silver glitter and stuck on stars.

Pattern pieces required: Crown 4A, medium and small star templates (see page 120).
Cutting list: From silver card cut one 4A, two medium and four small stars. (Measure around doll's head and adjust circumference if necessary.)

Making up
- Run a line of silver glitter along the top shaped edge of the crown.
- Paint glitter on to the face side of all stars.
- Glue stars to the five points and centre front as shown.
- Glue crown together at the back to fit doll's head.
- Glue two 2.5cm (1in) loops of narrow ribbon to either side of crown. This will enable the crown to be held in place using kirby grips (bobby pins).

Magic wand

No good fairy is complete without her magic wand and Glinda's is made from a silver glittering star glued to a chopstick.

Cutting list: From silver card cut one large star.

Making up
- Paint silver glitter on the face side of the star.
- Cut chopstick to 18cm (7in) and paint with silver paint.
- When dry, glue the star to the tip of the chopstick.

Slippers

Glinda's slippers are little slip-ons made from pink velveteen with silver buckles and stars decorating the toes.

Pattern pieces required: Slipper upper 4K, Slipper sole 4L.
Cutting list: From velveteen cut two 4K.
From pink satin cut two 4K and two 4L (one reversed).

Making up
- Iron interfacing to the satin soles.
- With right sides facing, stitch the upper and lining together around the top inner edge only. Trim and clip curves.
- Open lining out and with right sides facing, stitch across the back. Open out seam, turn upper down over lining and stay stitch close to the edge, all around the upper inner edge.
- Run a gathering stitch by hand around the outer edge of the upper starting and finishing at the back seam. Pull up slightly to form a rounded toe.
- Turn upper wrong side out and tack to sole before stitching. Turn right side out. Thread ribbon through buckle and glue to slipper.

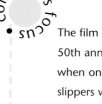

collector's focus

The film was just short of its 50th anniversary in June 1988 when one pair of the ruby slippers worn by Judy Garland sold for a record US$165,000 at Christie's. They were covered in rouge silk, had a rhinestone trimmed bow on each shoe, and were topped off with 2,300 crimson sequins.

What's underneath?

Dorothy's underwear consists of panties, petticoat and ankle socks. Glinda is wearing a self-lined camisole made from cotton lawn with ribbon straps and lace edging at the top. It fastens at the back with tiny snap fasteners. The full bloomers have a waistband and gather at the legs with a ruffle. Her half-petticoat is made from two fully gathered layers of pink netting finished at the bottom with netting ruffles and lace edging. The waistline is gathered into an elastic band.

you will need

20cm (8in) print calico

⅓ metre/yard white cotton lawn or batiste

⅔ metre/yard pink netting

Assorted ribbon and lace trimmings

Lightweight iron-on interfacing

6mm (¼in) wide flat elastic

2 buttons

12mm (½in) wide flat elastic

3 snap fasteners

Socks made from stretch cotton (see page 12)

Instructions

Dorothy's panties

The panties are made from one piece of calico. They have an elasticized waist and lace trim at the leg openings.

Pattern pieces required: Panties 3R.
Cutting list: From print calico cut one 3R.

Making up

- Run a line of stay stitching around the leg openings 3mm ($\frac{1}{8}$in) from the edge. Clip the curve up to the stay stitching and press the raw edge over the stitching to the wrong side. Turn in another 3mm ($\frac{1}{8}$in) and hand stitch in place using tiny stitches.
- Hand stitch lace trim at the hem.
- With right sides facing, stitch the sides together and zigzag raw edges to finish.
- Cut a length of narrow elastic the size of the doll's waist less 12mm ($\frac{1}{2}$in) and stitch the ends together forming a circle. Zigzag stitch along the top edge of the panties. With the circle of elastic inside the panties, turn down 6mm ($\frac{1}{2}$in) and stitch all the way around to form a casing.

Dorothy's petticoat

The petticoat buttons at the shoulders and has a simple lace trim at the hemline.

Pattern pieces required: Petticoat front 3S, Petticoat back 3T, Front facing 3Y, Back facing 3Z.
Cutting list: From cotton lawn cut one 3S, one 3T, one 3Y, and one 3Z.

Making up

- With right sides facing, stitch petticoat front and back together at sides and facing front and back together at sides. Press seams open.
- Finish bottom edge of facing using a zigzag stitch. With right sides facing, stitch petticoat and facing together around top edges. Trim, turn to right side and press.
- Turn a 3mm ($\frac{1}{8}$in) hem at the bottom and add lace trim.

- Work buttonholes on back straps where indicated and sew buttons to front straps.

Glinda's camisole

Choose narrow ribbon and lace to make the straps and to decorate the edge of the camisole.

Pattern pieces required: Camisole bodice front 4E, Camisole bodice back 4F.

Cutting list: From cotton lawn cut two 4E and four 4F (two reversed). Iron lightweight interfacing to one set of bodice front and backs before cutting out.

Making up

- With right sides facing, stitch the interfaced bodice front and backs together at sides. Repeat for lining. Press seams open.
- Stitch ribbon trim to bodice front where indicated. Stitch down both sides of ribbon.
- Tack lace to right side of bodice along top edge with the lace facing downwards.
- Measure ribbon straps for length and cut. Pin to bodice backs where indicated. Ribbon should be facing downwards.
- With right sides facing, lay the lining over the bodice and stitch all the way around, sandwiching lace and straps (be careful not to catch the end of the straps in the lower stitching) and leaving the left side open for turning. Trim, turn, stitch opening and press.
- Tie a ribbon bow and stitch on.

Glinda's bloomers

The bloomers are gathered just below the knee and two tiny bows decorate the front of each leg.

Pattern pieces required: Bloomers 4G.
Cutting list: From cotton lawn cut two 4G (one reversed) and one waistband to fit doll's waist plus 2.5cm (1in) by 5cm (2in).

Making up

- Press up 6mm ($\frac{1}{4}$in) at the bottom of each leg. Turn up another 6mm ($\frac{1}{4}$in) and stitch in place.

- Measure round doll's leg just below the knee and mark the measurement on the narrow elastic. Stitch elastic to bloomer legs where indicated, using zigzag stitch and pulling up on the elastic until the mark hits the other side. Cut off elastic end and repeat for other leg.
- With right sides facing, stitch fronts together and backs together leaving 7.5cm (3in) open from the top on the back. Stitch each leg together across crotch. Finish seam edges with zigzag stitch.
- Iron lightweight interfacing to the waistband and set to waistline allowing one end to overlap (see page 11). Work a buttonhole and sew on button.
- Tie two tiny ribbon bows and stitch to the front of each leg over the elastic.

Glinda's half-petticoat

The petticoat is made from two layers of netting gathered together at the waist. The top layer has a ruffle made from netting around the bottom.

Cutting list: Cut four rectangles of netting 25cm (10in) by 137cm (54in) and four ruffles 10cm (4in) by 137cm (54in).

Making up
- Stitch two petticoat rectangles together at one short end. Trim to stitching. Repeat for remaining two rectangles. On one petticoat set, run a line of stitching 5cm (2in) up from the bottom edge.
- Stitch the short end of all four ruffles together to make a long strip. Trim seams to stitching.

With wrong sides facing, fold ruffle in half lengthwise and run two rows of gathering stitches 6mm ($\frac{1}{4}$in) below the folded edge.
- Pin and stitch the ruffle to the right side of the petticoat using the line of stitching as a guideline, pulling up on and adjusting the gathers evenly. Stitch decorative lace edging over the ruffle.
- With wrong sides facing, put the plain petticoat inside the ruffled petticoat matching the seams and stay stitch the two together at the top. Zigzag the top edge to finish. Now run two rows of gathering stitches just below the stitching and pull up to about 46cm (18in). Cut a length of 12mm ($\frac{1}{2}$in) flat elastic to fit doll's waist less 2.5cm (1in) and stitch to the very edge of the petticoat over the zigzagging, pulling up on the elastic. The elastic should fit across the top of the petticoat. Pull out the gathering stitches.

In 1939 the film *The Wizard of Oz* won an Academy Award for Best Song, *Over the Rainbow*, but lost Best Picture to *Gone With the Wind*. Executives at MGM were nervous about 16-year-old Judy Garland playing Dorothy, despite her appearing in 14 other films, but her singing voice won her the part. She even won a Special Award for Outstanding Juvenile Performance in the shape of a Munchkin-sized Oscar.

- With right sides facing, fold the petticoat in half and stitch across elasticized waistband and down to the bottom of the petticoat. Trim the netting to the seam.

'I'll think about that tomorrow... after all, tomorrow is another day.'

Gone with the Wind

Set in America's Deep South during the Civil War, Margaret Mitchell's story centres on the beautiful but wilful Scarlett O'Hara and her infatuation with her neighbour, Ashley Wilkes. After her father's death, determined to hold on to Tara the family plantation, Scarlett marries Rhett Butler, an arrogantly charming profiteer. When Scarlett finally realizes that she loves Rhett it is too late and she loses him.

The doll shown is a reproduction of the German Mein Liebling (My Darling) from the author's collection. She stands 61cm (24in) high.

Scarlett O'Hara

'Oh, fiddle-dee-dee!'

This outfit fits a 58–63cm (23–25in) doll.

you will need

1.15 metre/1¼ yard cotton batiste in a spring green floral design

33cm (13in) by 20cm (8in) dark green velvet

Small amount of cotton lining fabric

1 metre/yard dark green narrow satin ribbon

Dark green thread

4 snap fasteners

2 small black beads

⅔ metre/yard green silk polyester or taffeta

Medium weight iron-on interfacing

1.3 metre (48in) of 6mm (¼in) dark green ribbon

Glue or glue gun

Chopstick

A straw hat (available at good craft or doll shops)

102cm (40in) of 2.5cm (1in) wide green ribbon

Margaret Mitchell was born in 1900. Her mother was a suffragette whose feminist ideas Margaret adopted, sometimes conflicting with her conservative father, a prominent lawyer. *Gone with the Wind* took ten years to write. Published in 1936, it sold more than 50,000 copies on the first day. In 1937 *Gone with the Wind* was awarded the Pulitzer Prize for Literature. The book has been translated into 25 languages.

Instructions

Barbecue dress

Scarlett O'Hara is off to the barbecue in her beautiful spring green dress that has a low cut bodice and three rows of self-fabric ruffles edged in dark green and trimmed with bows. The full skirt is six times the doll's waistline and held out by a hooped petticoat. A dark green velvet belt is attached to the self-lined bodice and the dress fastens at the back with four snap fasteners.

Pattern pieces required: Bodice front 5V, Bodice back 5W, Yoke front 5X, Yoke back 5Y, Belt 5Z.

Cutting list: From cotton batiste cut two 5V, four 5W (two reversed), two 5X, four 5Y (two reversed), one 5Z, three ruffles 86cm (34in) long by 5cm (2in) wide and a dirndl skirt six times the doll's waist measurement by waist to foot measurement plus 7.5cm (3in). (The skirt is longer as the hooped petticoat holds it out.) From velvet cut one 5Z.

Making up

• Work darts in bodice back and press towards the centre. Repeat for lining.

• Stitch front and back yokes together at shoulders. Press seams open. Repeat for lining.

• Stitch bodice front and backs together down sides. Repeat for lining. With right sides facing, stitch bodice and lining together under arms and down back openings. Trim, turn and press.

• With right sides facing, stitch yoke and yoke lining together at the sides. Turn and press. Overlock the bottom edge of the yoke and the lining separately. Sandwich bodice front between yoke and lining, matching notches, and stitch in place.

• Using a tiny zigzag stitch overcast one long edge of each ruffle.

Have you ever wondered why there were so many green costumes in *Gone with the Wind*? It was Margaret Mitchell's favourite colour.

Change to the dark green thread, overcasting at least three more times for a nice solid border. Trim off any frayed threads, turn the ends in 6mm (¼in) and hand stitch. Press. If your machine does not have a zigzag stitch, topstitch very narrow green ribbon to the edge of the ruffles.

• Gather all three ruffles separately and stitch to yoke, one at top edge, one where yoke meets bodice and

one in between. Distribute the gathers evenly. Finish stitching the top two ruffles 12mm (½in) from the back left, leaving space for snap fastener placement.

- Cut a length of self-fabric on the bias about 2.5cm (1in) wide to fit around the neck edge plus 6mm (¼in) at each end. Press one side in 6mm (¼in) and with right sides facing, stitch the raw edge of the bias strip to the neck edge covering the raw edge of the first ruffle. Fold in ends, fold the bias strip over and hand stitch in place.

- Make a dirndl skirt (see page 11) and attach it to the bodice only. Turn the bodice lining over the skirt, turn up the raw edge and hand stitch in place.

- With right sides facing, stitch the belt and lining together all the way around leaving a 5cm (2in) opening on the straight edge, opposite the point. Trim corners, turn, close up the opening and press. Pin the belt to the dress with the point facing up and hand stitch in place.

- Turn a 2.5cm (1in) hem at the bottom and hand stitch. Sew snap fasteners to the back where indicated (one on the belt) and add five ribbon bows as shown.

Slippers

To match the belt on her dress Scarlett is wearing a pair of green velvet slippers.

Pattern pieces required: Slipper upper 6D, Slipper sole 6E.
Cutting list: From velvet cut two 6D and two 6E (one reversed). From contrasting cotton lining fabric cut two 6D.

Making up
- With right sides facing, stitch the upper and lining together around the inner top edge only. Trim and clip curves.
- Open lining out and with right sides facing, stitch across the back of upper and lining. Open out seam, turn upper down over lining and stay stitch through both layers all around the upper, close to the edge.
- Run a gathering stitch by hand around the toe of the upper and pull up slightly to round the toe. Turn wrong side out and tack to sole before stitching. Turn right side out.
- Stitch narrow satin or velvet ribbon to inside of upper where indicated. Try shoe on doll for

strap length, sew other end on the outside where indicated. Add beads and satin ribbon bows.

Sunbonnet

A large straw hat with wide green ribbon ties will keep the bright sunshine out of Scarlett's eyes.

Making up
- Cut two ribbons, 50cm (20in) long, and glue to each side of the bonnet inside the crown.
- Cut the ends of the ribbon at an angle. Dab a tiny bit of glue along each cut end to stop them fraying.

Parasol

Scarlett's pretty green parasol was an indispensable fashion accessory. It not only complemented her outfit but also protected her peaches and cream complexion from the sun. Sometimes she may have used it as an instrument of propriety to ward off the unwanted attentions of the opposite sex.

Cutting list: From silk polyester cut two circles 30cm (12in) in diameter, one strip 2 metres/2⅛ yards long by 10cm (4in) wide, and one strip 25cm (10in) long by 6cm (2½in) wide.

Making up
- Iron a 2.5cm (1in) diameter circle of interfacing to the wrong side of the centre of each fabric circle.
- With right sides facing, stitch the two fabric circles together 6mm (¼in) from the outer edge, leaving a small opening for turning. Trim, turn to right side, turn the raw

edges of the opening in and topstitch all the way around the circumference. Press.
- Topstitch across the circle to create six symmetrical wedges. Fig 1.

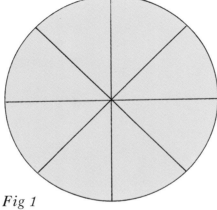

Fig 1

- Using an awl, poke a hole through the centre of the circle where the lines intersect. Keeping the hole small and tight, neaten around the edge using buttonhole stitch (see page 9). Fig 2.

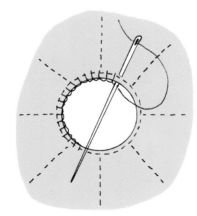

Fig 2

- Stitch the long fabric strip together at the ends using a run and fell seam (see page 9), and finish both sides with a tight zigzag stitch.
- Run two rows of gathering stitches starting 2.5cm (1in) from one side

of the strip. Pull the gathers up, pin to the edge of the circle with the larger edge of the ruffle facing out, distribute the gathers evenly and stitch in place between the gathers. Pull out the gathering stitches carefully.
- Push the small end of the chopstick through the eyelet so it protrudes about 2.5cm (1in), then dab a bit of glue around the hole from the inside.
- Make the smaller fabric strip into a ruffle in the same way as the large but only run one row of gathering stitches down the centre, pull up snugly and tie off. Push the ruffle over the end of the chopstick at the top and glue it in place.
- Gather up the fabric of the parasol evenly and hold in place with a ribbon tied in a bow just above the ruffle as shown.

did you know?

Margaret Mitchell had a devoted interest in Atlanta's African–American community. She was the only one in her debutante group at Smith College who chose to work in the city's black clinics. For many years she contributed to a scholarship fund that enabled 50 black students to graduate from medical college and she also supported the efforts to de-segregate the city's police department.

The doll shown is a modern Ivan doll.
He is 63cm (25in) high.

Rhett Butler

'No, I don't think I will kiss you, although you need kissing badly.'

This outfit fits a 58–63cm (23–25in) doll.

you will need

½ metre/yard polyester linen

½ metre/yard lining fabric

¼ metre/yard cotton batiste

30cm (12in) cotton print or raw silk for the cravat

¼ metre/yard brocade

5 buttons covered in brocade

8 shirt buttons

5 jacket buttons

Lightweight iron-on interfacing

Narrow seam binding

Small amount of decorative cording

Tiepin or pearl shank button

23cm (9in) square of cream felt

Medium weight card

Glue or glue gun

25cm (10in) square black leather

Small length of narrow black ribbon

Black paint

Instructions

Shirt

Rhett's fitted shirt is made from cotton batiste with long cuffed sleeves and a high collar with points that turn down over a stylish printed cravat. The fullness of the sleeves is reduced by two neat tucks.

Pattern pieces required: Shirt front 6Q, Shirt back 6R, Shirt sleeve 6S, Shirt collar 6T, Shirt cuff 6U.

Cutting list: From batiste cut two 6Q (one reversed), one 6R, two 6S, two 6T and four 6U (two reversed). Iron lightweight iron-on interfacing to one side of collar, one side of cuffs and down shirt facings.

Making up

- With right sides facing, stitch collars together leaving neck edge open. Trim, turn and press. Repeat for cuffs, stitching along curved and short edges.
- Work darts in shirt back tapering the points. Press darts to centre back. With right sides facing, stitch fronts and back together at shoulders using a run and fell seam (see page 9). Press.
- Work bound openings at sleeves remembering to reverse one (see page 11). Run two rows of gathering stitches at the top of sleeves and set using Method 2 (see page 11) using a run and fell seam as before.
- Fold back two 6mm (¼in) tucks on the top side of the sleeve, just in

front of the bound opening with the folds towards the opening. Pin the tucks in place, turn back the bound opening at the top of the sleeve and follow instructions for setting cuffs (see page 11). Set the cuff at the edge of both sides of the sleeve. Fig 1.

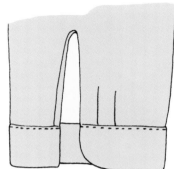

Fig 1

- Turn the front facing edges of the shirt in 3mm (⅛in) and topstitch in place.
- With right sides facing, stitch underside of collar to shirt. Turn the facings back over the entire collar and stitch up to the ends of the facing, leaving the centre of the top collar free. Trim the corners and the seam allowance up to the ends of the facings. At these two points snip up to the stitching and press seam allowance well up into the collar. Turn in the remaining raw edge and hand stitch in place. Hand stitch the rest of the facings down and press.
- Finish the shirt tail by zigzagging the edge then turning it up 3mm (⅛in) and stitching in place.
- Press the points of the collar down so they stick out when the shirt is on the doll.
- Work buttonholes where indicated and sew on buttons.

Waistcoat

Rhett's single-breasted waistcoat is made in a brocade that matches the suiting. The buttons are covered in self-fabric.

Pattern pieces required: Waistcoat front 6V, Waistcoat back 6W.

Cutting list: From brocade cut two 6V (one reversed), one 6W and one welt 4.5cm (1¾in) by 6cm (2¼in). From lining fabric cut two 6V (one reversed) and one 6W.

Making up

- With right sides facing, fold long side of welt in half and stitch sides together. Trim corners and turn.

Zigzag raw edges of welt together and press. On the left side of waistcoat, place welt upside down along lower line, and stitch across zigzag edge where indicated and 12mm (½in) above. Fig 2. Turn welt down over stitching and tack at lower corners.

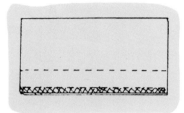

Fig 2

- With right sides facing, stitch fronts and back together at shoulders. Press seams open. Repeat for lining. Stitch the waistcoat and lining together around the neck and down the fronts to where indicated and around the armholes. Trim, notch curves and turn through to right side. Press.
- Open out the lining from the waistcoat and with right sides facing, stitch down the sides of lining and waistcoat. Press the seams open, turn the waistcoat over the lining and press again.

- Press 6mm (¼in) up around the bottom of the waistcoat and lining separately and hand stitch closed using a blind stitch (see page 9).
- Cover five buttons with self-fabric, following manufacturer's instructions. Work buttonholes and sew on buttons.

Jacket

The jacket and trousers of Rhett's suit are made from polyester linen to resemble suiting, which would prove too bulky for construction on such a small scale. The long fitted jacket closes with one button.

Pattern pieces required: Jacket front 6F, Jacket back 6G, Jacket sleeve 6H, Jacket collar 6I, Jacket front facing 6J, Jacket back facing 6K, Jacket front lining 6L and Jacket back lining 6M.

Cutting list: From linen cut two 6F (one reversed), two 6G (one reversed), two 6H (one reversed), two 6I, two 6J (one reversed), one 6K and two welts each 5cm (2in) by 5cm (2in).

From lining fabric cut two 6L (one reversed), two 6M (one reversed) and two 6H (one reversed).

The front and back facings and two collar pieces are interfaced with lightweight iron-on interfacing (see pattern piece).

Making up

- Work and stitch welts to both sides of jacket front where indicated following the instructions for waistcoat welts given left.
- With right sides facing, stitch jacket backs together from neck to indication mark. Press open seam and down back openings.
- With right sides facing, stitch fronts and back together at shoulders and down sides.
- Repeat these two steps for lining. Press 6mm (¼in) up at the bottom of the lining.
- Stitch back and front facings together at ends matching notches. Press seams open. Stitch 6mm (¼in) in around the outside edge (not the bottom ends).
- With right sides facing, stitch both collar pieces together leaving bottom edge open for turning. Trim, clip corners, turn and press.
- Pin completed collar to right side of jacket between indication marks and tack in place. Pin right side of facings over collar, down jacket fronts and stitch all the way around including the bottom ends. Trim, clip corners, turn and press. Press up lower jacket edge to match facing ends.

- Stitch seam binding to wrist end of sleeves. Run zigzag stitch along wrist end of sleeve linings.
- Run two rows of gathering stitches at top of sleeves between indication marks. With right sides facing, stitch sleeves together at sides and set using Method 1 (see page 10). Repeat for lining.
- With wrong sides facing, pull the jacket lining over the jacket and tack together at the side seams just under the sleeve, the shoulder seams at the top of the sleeve and the back seam at the top of the lining. Turn the facing over the lining, and blind hem. Hem the lining over the pressed up bottom edge of the jacket.
- Turn the sleeve ends up and hem. Do not catch the lining.
- Work one buttonhole on the front with its matching button and sew two buttons on each sleeve where indicated.

Breeches

Under his frock coat Rhett wears the tight fitting breeches that were fashionable at the time. A pair of stirrups made out of black elastic hook under the foot.

Pattern pieces required: Breeches front/back 6N, Turn-up 6P.

Cutting list: From polyester linen cut two 6N (one reversed) and two 6P (one reversed). The breeches are cut higher at the front of the foot and come lower at the heel, so when cutting out, cut both legs for the back then open them out and cut the fronts where indicated.

Making up

- Work darts in back of breeches and press towards the centre. With right sides facing, stitch fronts together and backs together from waist to crotch.
- Cut two lengths of 12mm (½in) elastic 'stirrups' about 8cm (3in) long. Pin one length of the elastic to the centre of the bottom edge of each leg of the breeches and with right sides facing, stitch turn-ups to each leg sandwiching the elastic. Zigzag stitch along the lower edge of the turn-up.
- With right sides facing, stitch legs together and across the turn-ups. Press seams open, fold turn-ups up into breeches and hand stitch in place.
- Zigzag the waistline edge and turn it down 12mm (½in) and hand stitch. Stitch around the back opening. Press.
- Try breeches on doll with shoes, pull stirrup under shoe to determine length. Stitch end of stirrup to inside of breeches at the seam.
- Sew a snap fastener at the back waistline and press creases down the front of breeches.

Cravat

The cravat is tied around the neck by looping one end over the other. Tuck the ends into the waistcoat

then 'blouse' it up and secure by sewing on the pearl button or alternatively use a tiepin.

Pattern pieces required: Cravat 7C.
Cutting list: From cotton print or raw silk cut two 7C.

Making up

- With right sides facing, stitch cravat pieces together all the way around leaving one end open for turning. Trim, turn and press.
- Hand stitch the opening closed.

When Macmillan published *Gone with the Wind* in 1936, the price of the book was US$3.00. Today a first edition is worth up to US$16,000.

Panama hat

A Panama hat made from the same fabric as the suit completes Rhett's gentlemanly appearance.

Pattern pieces required: Panama hat brim A 6X, Panama hat brim B 6Y, Panama side crown 6Z, Panama top crown A 7A and Panama top crown B 7B.

Cutting list: From linen cut one 6X, one 6Y, one 6Z (cut the top edge 6mm (¼in) higher than the pattern piece and don't cut the notches at this time), one 7A and one 7B. From felt cut one 6X and one 7A. From card cut two 6X, one 6Z (don't cut the notches at this time), and two 7A.

Making up

- Glue the side crown card and fabric together, turn and glue the fabric over the top edge of the card then cut out the notches.
- Glue felt pieces to card brim A and one top crown A.

- Run a row of gathering stitches on fabric brim B where indicated. Place brim B over felt side of brim A and glue together around centre opening only. When glue has set, pull up firmly on the gathers and tie off underneath the brim. Glue under the gathered edge of the fabric. Fig 3.

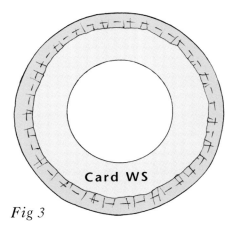

Card WS

Fig 3

- Take the side crown, form it into a ring, check to make sure it will push through the hole of the brim snugly then glue the edges in place. When the glue has set, push the side crown inside the brim, fold the tabs to the underside and glue in place. (A glue gun works very quickly, but use it sparingly.)
- Trim 6mm (¼in) from the outside edge of the second card brim A and glue over the gathered edges of the fabric-covered brim. Now glue the remaining fabric brim A over the card to finish.
- Run a row of gathering stitches on fabric top crown B where indicated and fix to the felt-covered side of top crown A as you did with the brim. Cover the gathered edges with fabric top crown A to finish.
- Glue the completed top crown to the top of the side crown.

- Tie decorative cording around the hat in a bow and knot the ends to prevent it unravelling.

Boots

Pattern pieces required: Toe 7I, Upper 7J, Sole 7K, Inner sole 7L, Heel 7M.

Cutting list: From leather cut two 7I, four 7J (two reversed), and two 7K (one reversed).
From card cut two 7K, two 7L and twelve 7M.

Making up

- With right sides facing, stitch uppers together at the back. Open out the seam and topstitch each side open. Stitch the fronts together, then starting at the toe end (widest end) stitch seam open.
- Glue toe to uppers. When glue has dried, topstitch across the upper edge of the toe for extra strength.
- Stitch a loop of ribbon to the back of the boot on the inside as shown.
- Run a line of stitching 6mm (¼in) in around the lower edge of the upper. Cut notches, attach soles and follow the basic instructions (see page 12).
- Glue six heels together forming one 6mm (¼in) high heel. Smooth it with a little sandpaper. Paint the heels black and glue to the sole.

What's underneath?

Scarlett's underwear consists of a lace-trimmed corset, pantalets and a hooped petticoat. Rhett's underwear is simply a one-piece pair of long johns that button up the front and have a mock flap at the seat.

you will need

¼ metre/yard cotton poplin

¼ metre/yard taffeta

2½ metres/3 yards boning

1½ metres/yards decorative flat lace

2½ metres/3 yards bias tape

76cm (30in) of 12mm (½in) wide satin ribbon

1 metre/yard of 6mm (¼in) wide satin ribbon

12 eyelets and tool (optional)

Decorative motif

Seed pearls

6mm (¼in) wide flat elastic

Various laces, trims and ribbons

⅔ metres/yards stretch cotton flannel

6 buttons

Instructions

Scarlett's corset

This self-lined corset is boned and laces up the back. There is a decorative lace edging along the top and bottom of the corset.

Pattern pieces required: Corset front 6A, Corset side 6B, Corset back 6C.

did you know?

It took two years to cast the film role of Scarlett O'Hara. Among the many actresses screen tested were Tallulah Bankhead, Susan Hayward, Paulette Goddard and Lana Turner. Producer David O Selznick finally found his Scarlett in British actress, Vivian Leigh. There was never any doubt as to who would play Rhett Butler – heart throb Clark Gable! The film won eight Academy Awards including Best Actress for Vivian Leigh.

Cutting list: From cotton poplin cut two 6A, four 6B (two reversed) and four 6C (two reversed).

Making up

- With right sides facing, stitch the sides to the front matching notches. Stitch the backs to the sides matching notches. Repeat for lining. Press seams towards the sides.
- Hand stitch decorative motif to centre front and embellish with seed pearls.
- With right sides facing, stitch lining and corset together down the backs and along the bottom edge to indication mark.

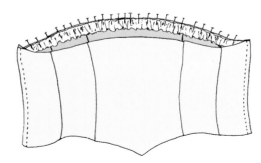

Fig 1

Pin tightly ruffled lace between the lining and the corset along the top edge, and stitch in place across the top. Fig 1. Trim corners, turn to right side and press.

- Press 6mm (¼in) up at the bottom of corset and lining.
- To make channels for boning, topstitch the corset and lining together down all four side seams and along the side of each seam where indicated. Push boning up the channels, cut off and tuck ends under the pressed up edge of the corset. The boning should fit snugly. Hand stitch the lining to the corset then hand stitch more lace to the top side of the bottom edge as shown.
- Fix eyelets down backs where indicated or make holes using an awl and work buttonhole stitches around the holes (see page 9). Lace satin ribbon through the eyelets, starting at the top, and tie in a bow at the bottom.

Scarlett's pantalets

Scarlett wears a pair of full-length pantalets under her hooped petticoat. The ends of the legs are decorated with eyelet lace threaded with ribbon.

Pattern pieces required: Pantalets 1Z.
Cutting list: From cotton poplin cut two 1Z (one reversed).

Making up
- Work as for Alice's drawers (see page 25).
- Decorate bottom of legs with lace and ribbon.

Hooped petticoat

The petticoat has two rows of boning to hold out the very full skirt of the dress. It is attached with ties around her waist.

Cutting list: From taffeta cut one dirndl skirt 137cm (1½ yards) wide by 38cm (15in) long.

Making up

- With right sides facing, stitch the sides together leaving a 8cm (3in) opening at the top. Press the seam open.
- Stitch bias tape to the right side of the skirt around the bottom edge. Stitch both edges of the tape creating a channel for the boning, leaving a small opening in one side to insert it. Stitch flat lace over the top edge of the bias tape to hide it. Stitch another channel of bias tape to the wrong side of the skirt, 8cm (3in) above the first channel.
- Run two rows of gathering stitches along the top and pull up to fit doll's waist. Bind the raw edge with 12mm (½in) wide ribbon and stitch in place leaving ribbon ties at both ends.
- Feed boning through the two channels so they fit snugly and hand stitch the openings closed.

Rhett's long johns

Made from flannel, the long johns are a one-piece garment which buttons down the front. A mock flap at the back is held up with two buttons.

Pattern pieces required: Front/back 7D, Front facing 7E, Back facing 7F, Sleeve 7G and Flap 7H.
Cutting list: From stretch cotton flannel cut two 7D (one reversed), two 7E (one reversed), one 7F, two 7G and one 7H.

Making up

- With right sides facing, stitch front and back facings together at shoulders. Turn 6mm (¼in) in around the outside of facing and stitch in place. Press seams open.

- With right sides facing, stitch fronts together from crotch to indication mark. Clip at top of stitching where indicated. Stitch backs together from crotch to neck. Stitch front and back together at shoulders. Press seams open.
- With right sides facing, stitch facing to long johns around neck and down fronts. Turn bottom edge of left side up 6mm (¼in), turn facing over long johns and hand stitch all the way around. Overlap the right side and topstitch across the bottom ends.
- With right sides facing, fold the flap in half and stitch down both sides. Trim, turn, press and stitch the open end closed. Lay the flap upside-down where indicated and

stitch in place. Fig 1. Sew flap closed using two buttons. Fig 2.
- Set sleeves using Method 2 (see page 11) continuing side seam down the length of the leg.
- With right sides facing, stitch legs together across the crotch.
- Turn up 6mm (¼in) hems at the leg and the sleeve ends and hand stitch in place.
- Work buttonholes where indicated down the front and sew on four matching buttons.

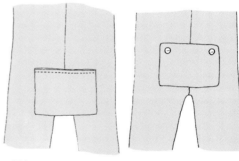

Fig 1   *Fig 2*

One of the dresses that Vivian Leigh wore for her role as Scarlett O'Hara sold for US$90,000 to the owner of a restaurant called Scarlett in Sao Paulo, Brazil.

Anne of Green Gables

The heart-rending story of *Anne of Green Gables*, by L M Montgomery, paints an emotional picture of Anne, an orphaned girl with decidedly red hair and a fiery temper who is fostered by an elderly brother and sister living at Green Gables, Prince Edward Island. Anne meets Diana, who becomes her 'bosom friend' and 'kindred spirit', and discovers life and love through a series of incidents and accidents while growing into a sensitive and compassionate young woman.

'Some people go through life trying to find out what the world holds for them only to find out too late that it's what they bring to the world that really counts.'

The doll shown is a Dianna Effner design from the author's collection. She is 48cm (19in) high.

Anne

'Oh, do you think you can like me a little... enough to be my bosom friend?'

This outfit fits a 43–48cm (17–19in) doll.

you will need

½ metre/yard calico in a tiny print

¼ metre/yard calico in a contrast plain colour or with a tiny stripe

7 buttons

Lightweight iron-on interfacing

8 tea bags

About 20cm (8in) by 30cm (12in) old or distressed leather

Brown or black crochet thread

30cm (12in) square woven cotton jacquard or tapestry fabric

16.5cm (6½in) by 5cm (2in) leather

23cm (9in) zip

Medium weight card

A straw hat (available from good craft or doll shops)

A length of grosgrain (petersham) ribbon to tie around hat

Instructions

Smock dress

Anne's smock dress has a Peter Pan collar, long sleeves with buttoned cuffs and a dirndl skirt. The bodice is self-lined and buttons at the back. The print calico was stained using tea bags before cutting out to achieve an old and worn look. See instructions on page 56 for tea staining.

Pattern pieces required: Bodice front 4M, Bodice back 4N, Collar 4P, Sleeve 4Q.

There are many similarities between the author and Anne. Lucy Maud Montgomery's grandparents raised her from a toddler after her mother's death. She was one of the few women of her time to seek higher education, studying English literature at Dalhousie University, Nova Scotia. She graduated with honours in one year, then became a teacher. After her grandfather died, Lucy went home to care for her grandmother for 13 years.

Cutting list: From print calico cut two 4M, four 4N (two reversed), four 4P (two reversed), two 4Q (one reversed), two cuffs 10cm (4in) by 5cm (2in) and one skirt 91.5cm (36in) by 25cm (10in).
One side of collar and cuffs are interfaced with lightweight iron-on interfacing before cutting out.

Making up
- With right sides facing, stitch bodice front and backs together at shoulders. Press seams open. Repeat for lining.
- With right sides facing, stitch the interfaced collar pieces to the non-interfaced pieces around the curved edge, leaving the neck edge open. Trim, turn and press. With right sides facing, centre and pin the collar pieces to the bodice neckline and stitch in place. The interfaced side should be on top.
- With right sides facing, pin the lining over the bodice, sandwiching the collar. Stitch up one side of the back, around the neckline and

down the other side. Trim corners, notch neckline, turn and press. From this point the bodice and lining are worked as one piece.
- Zigzag the edges of the lining to the bodice at side fronts, around the sleeve openings and down the side backs to keep them together.
- Work bound sleeve openings in sleeves (see page 11).
- Run two rows of gathering stitches at the top of the sleeves and set using Method 2 (see page 11).
- Set cuff (see page 11).
- With right sides facing, fold skirt in half and stitch together leaving 7.5cm (3in) open at the top. Press seam open. Turn 6mm (¼in) up at the bottom and press. Run two rows of gathering stitches at the top and pull up gathers.
- With right sides facing, pin skirt to bodice adjusting the gathers. Stitch in place. Press seam allowance up and topstitch along seam line to hold.
- Turn up a further 2.5cm (1in) at skirt bottom and hand hem. Press.
- Work buttonholes at the back where indicated and at the cuffs. Sew on buttons to match.

Pinafore

The pinafore has a self-lined yoke that buttons at the back. The skirt is gathered where it is attached to the yoke and has two patch pockets.

Pattern pieces required: Yoke front 4R, Yoke back 4S, Armhole facing 4T, Skirt front 4U, Skirt back 4V, Pocket 4W.
Cutting list: From contrast/striped calico cut two 4R, four 4S (two reversed), two 4T (one reversed), one 4U, two 4V (one reversed) and two 4W.

Making up
- Turn down 6mm (¼in) at the top of the pocket and stitch. With right sides facing, turn the top of the pocket over 12mm (½in) and stitch together at the sides. Clip the top corners. Fig 1. Turn to right side. Press in 6mm (¼in) at the sides and bottom and pin to pinafore skirt front where indicated. Topstitch in place.

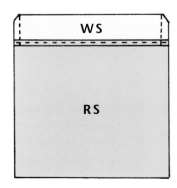

Fig 1

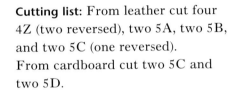

- With right sides facing, stitch pinafore skirt front and backs together at sides. Press seams open.
- Turn up 6mm (¼in) and stitch around outer curved edge of armhole facing. With right sides together, stitch facing to armholes in pinafore. Notch, turn, press and hand stitch facing to the pinafore.
- Turn and stitch a 6mm (¼in) hem down each side of the back.
- With right sides facing, stitch front and back yokes together at shoulders. Press seams open. Repeat for lining.
- Press interfacing to one yoke unit. With right sides facing, stitch yoke unit and interfaced yoke unit together around neckline, down the backs and around the armholes. Trim, turn through to right side and press.
- Run two rows of gathering stitches across the top front and backs of the skirt separately. Pull up stitches and with wrong side of skirt to right side of yoke lining, pin together, distributing the gathers evenly, and stitch in place. Turn raw edges of yoke front and backs up 6mm (¼in), pin over skirt and topstitch in place.
- Turn up and stitch 6mm (¼in) at the bottom of the skirt, then turn up 4cm (1½in) and hand hem. Press.
- Work two buttonholes on the back yoke where indicated and sew on buttons to match.

Tea staining

To tea stain about ½ metre/yard of cotton fabric, fill the kitchen sink half full with very hot water and add about eight tea bags (opened) or use loose tea. Mix the tea and allow it to steep for about five minutes before submerging the fabric. To stain the fabric evenly wet it first then layer it into the tea bath.

Allow the fabric to soak for about 30 minutes stirring frequently with a wooden spoon and keeping it under the water to make sure it is evenly saturated. (If you want an uneven, stained effect, crumple the fabric allowing bits to stick out of the water as it sets.) When you have reached the desired depth of colour, rinse the fabric in warm water, gently wring out the excess and hang it out to dry in the sun. Sunlight will help set the colour. Iron the fabric before cutting out.

Boots

If possible, use old and worn leather for the boots to simulate well-worn shoes. To distress new leather, rub it against the fine teeth of a food grater or a wood file, and dab on bleach sporadically to lift the colour.

Pattern pieces required: Upper 4Z, Toe 5A, Tongue 5B, Sole 5C, Inner sole 5D.

Cutting list: From leather cut four 4Z (two reversed), two 5A, two 5B, and two 5C (one reversed). From cardboard cut two 5C and two 5D.

Making up
- Use an awl to make holes in all boot uppers where indicated.
- With right sides facing, stitch pairs of uppers together from A to B. Open seam, lay the right side of the tongue over the open seam and stitch in place. Fig 2.

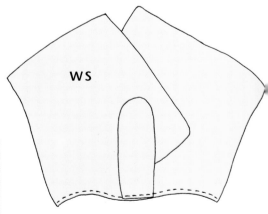

WS

Fig 2

did you know?

After completing *Anne of Green Gables* in 1905 the book was rejected by several publishers. L M Montgomery put the manuscript away in a hatbox and it wasn't until 1908 that she decided to try again, this time with success. The book became an immediate best seller and she went on to write 12 more books in the Anne series.

- Lay wrong side of toe over right side of uppers and topstitch in place. Fig 3.

Fig 3

- With right sides facing, stitch boots up the back, open out and stitch seam open.
- Follow basic instructions for soles (see page 12).
- Insert crochet thread into holes for laces.

Carpetbag

Carpet fabric would prove much too heavy for this small-scale bag with leather handles. If you can't find woven cotton jacquard you could use a lightweight tapestry, the kind used to cover throw cushions.

Pattern pieces required: Top 5E, Side 5F, End 5G.

Cutting list: From fabric cut two 5E, one 5F and two 5G.
From leather cut two strips 16.5cm (6½in) by 2.5cm (1in).
From card cut one piece 17cm (6¾in) by 5cm (2in).

Making up

- With right sides facing, stitch top pieces together lengthwise using a long stitch on your machine. Press the seam open and set the zip according to package instructions, centring it on the seam. Remove the long machine stitches.
- With right sides facing, stitch an end piece to each end of top to form one long unit. Trim seams and zigzag the edges to prevent the fabric from fraying.
- With right sides facing, stitch each end of the top unit to either side of the carpetbag between the marks indicated. Open the zip, pin the remaining edges around both sides of the carpetbag and stitch in place. Zigzag all raw edges and turn carpetbag right side out.

Collector's focus

L M Montgomery sold the rights of her first book to her American publisher who then published unauthorised versions of her subsequent books in America. She was involved in a nine-year court battle with them, which she eventually won.

- Roll and glue each leather strip into handles and when glue has dried, stitch the handles, with the cut edge underneath, to each side of the carpetbag where indicated.
- Insert the cardboard inside the bottom of the carpetbag.

Hat

After staining with tea, fray the edges of Anne's straw hat and add a ribbon round the brim.

Making up

- Tea stain the hat (see instructions in box above left).
- Dry the hat back into shape by placing it over a glass or jar the size of the doll's head and hold it in place with a rubber band until completely dry.
- When dry, fray the edges for a worn look.
- Glue ribbon around the crown and tie at the back.

The doll shown is a Dianna Effner portrait head #1 design from the author's collection. She is 48cm (19in) high.

Anne of Green Gables has been filmed three times, adapted as a stage musical, serialized on television and translated into 15 languages. Mark Twain, author of *Tom Sawyer*, described the book as 'the sweetest creation of child life yet written'.

Diana

'I'm awfully glad you've come to live at Green Gables. It will be jolly to have somebody to play with.'

This outfit fits a 43–48cm (17–19in) doll.

you will need

½ metre/yard pink polyester viscose

About 20cm (8in) white lace fabric

¼ metre/yard white cotton lawn

20cm (8in) of 2cm (1in) wide white lace edging

4½ metres/5 yards of 3mm (⅛in) wide pink satin ribbon

15cm (6in) of 1.5cm (⅝in) wide pink satin ribbon

9 snap fasteners

5 buttons

Pink seam binding

Lightweight iron-on interfacing

30cm (12in) square of cream leather

8 small boot or shank buttons

Medium weight cardboard

A straw boater (available from good craft or doll shops)

Various silk flowers in complementary colours

About 60cm (24in) velvet ribbon to go round hat and tie in a bow

Glue or glue gun

Instructions

Dress

Diana's pretty summer frock consists of a sleeveless dress made from a lace bodice stitched to a dirndl skirt made in pink fabric and trimmed with two rows of ribbon. A ruffle lace neck edging peeks out above her matching jacket.

Pattern pieces required: Bodice front 5H, Bodice back 5I.
Cutting list: From lace fabric cut one 5H and two 5I (one reversed). From cotton lawn cut one 5H and two 5I (one reversed). From polyester viscose cut one skirt twice the doll's waist measurement by 28cm (11in).

Making up

- With right sides facing, stitch lace bodice front and backs together at shoulders. Press seams open. Repeat for lining.
- Pin lace edging to right side of lining neck edge with pins at right angles and lace facing down. Then pin right side of lace bodice over, sandwiching the lace. Stitch around neckline and down the backs. Stitch around armholes. Trim, turn to right side and press.

- Open out bodice from lining and stitch down the sides. Open seams, turn bodice over lining and press. Stay stitch the bodice and lining together at the bottom. Zigzag stitch or overcast to stop fraying.

- With right sides facing, stitch skirt together at back leaving a 5cm (2in) opening at the top. Run two parallel rows of gathering stitches around top. With right sides facing, pin skirt to bodice pulling up and distributing gathers evenly and stitch in place. Press raw edges towards the bodice and topstitch in place.
- Stitch seam binding to the hemline and turn a 2.5cm (1in) hem, tack and press. On right side topstitch two rows of ribbon trim. The stitching should catch the seam binding on the other side, stitching the hem in place. Take out tacking and press.
- Work snap fasteners at the back where indicated.

Jacket

The short, lined jacket matches the skirt and buttons down the back. The wide lapel collar, sleeves and cuffs are trimmed with ribbon to match the skirt of the dress.

Pattern pieces required: Jacket front 5J, Jacket back 5K, Collar 5L, Sleeve 5M, Cuff 5N.
Cutting list: From polyester viscose cut one 5J, two 5K (one reversed), two 5L (one reversed), two 5M (one reversed) and two 5N. From lining fabric cut one 5J and two 5K (one reversed). One side of collar and cuffs are interfaced with lightweight iron-on interfacing before cutting out.

Making up

- With right sides facing, stitch jacket front and backs together at shoulders. Repeat for lining.
- On the interfaced side of the collar

pieces, using the narrow ribbon, topstitch two rows of ribbon where indicated. Start at the sides, then overlap them with ribbon across the front and back. With right sides facing, stitch top collar to under collar leaving the neck edge open. Trim, turn and press.
- Tack the collars to the jacket neckline matching the indication marks. Pin jacket lining over the collar and bodice and stitch around neckline and down backs. Trim, turn and press.
- With right sides facing, stitch front and backs together down sides and lining separately. Press seams open. Press up 6mm (¼in) at the bottom of the jacket and lining, pin them together and hand stitch using blind stitch (see page 9).
- Zigzag the bodice and lining together around the armholes.

- Topstitch ribbon trim to sleeves where indicated.
- With right sides facing, stitch sleeves together down sides. Press seams open. Work bound openings (see page 11).
- Make cuffs and set to sleeves (see page 11). Stitch ribbon trim to cuffs. The first row where cuff meets sleeve. The second row 1cm (⅜in) down. Turn ribbon ends over the cuff and hand stitch.
- Run two rows of gathering stitches at top of sleeves and set into bodice using Method 1 (see page 10).
- Work mock buttonholes at cuffs and back of jacket where indicated (see snap fasteners, page 9).
- Tie a reef knot in a wide piece of satin ribbon and hand stitch to front between collar pieces.

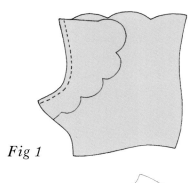

Fig 1

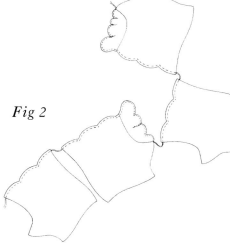

Fig 2

reversed), two 5T, two 5U (one reversed) and two 5C (one reversed).
From cardboard cut two 5C and two 5D.

Making up
- Measure buttons and make slits in flaps to correspond.
- Match flap to inside upper and with right sides facing, stitch from A to B. Fig 1. Clip seam allowance at curve, across seam allowance corners and trim.

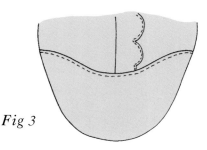

Fig 3

- Topstitch uppers across the tops and around the scalloped flaps. Work using an assembly line method. Fig 2.
- With right sides together stitch outside upper to inside upper from C to D and open out seam.
- Glue and topstitch wrong side of toe to right side of uppers. Fig 3.
- Follow basic shoe instructions to complete (see page 12).
- Sew on boot buttons.

Straw boater

Diana wears a straw boater ringed with velvet ribbon and silk flowers.

Making up
- Glue velvet ribbon around the crown and tie a bow at the back.
- Decorate the hat by gluing silk flowers on the front of the brim.

High-buttoned boots

The boots are made from cream coloured leather and have scalloped boot flaps. They button at the sides with pearl boot buttons.

Pattern pieces required: Inside upper 5R, Outside upper 5S, Toe 5T, Flap 5U, Sole 5C, and Inner sole 5D.
Cutting list: From leather cut two 5R (one reversed), two 5S (one

What's underneath?

Anne's underwear consists of standard orphanage issue vest and drawers while in complete contrast, Diana is wearing an embroidered silk camisole, a half-petticoat and bloomers that are worn over white stockings.

you will need

¼ metre/yard of cotton winceyette

Small amount of edging lace

A small amount of crêpe de chine (raw silk), preferably with a patterned border

Small amount of cotton lawn

38cm (15in) of 6mm (¼in) wide satin ribbon

Small amount of satin ribbon 3mm (⅛in) wide

25cm (10in) of 6mm (¼in) wide flat elastic

25cm (10in) of 1cm (⅜in) wide flat elastic

2 snap fasteners

Instructions

Anne's vest

The vest is made from winceyette, a knitted fabric that stretches when sewn. This characteristic can be used to create a simple scalloped edge. The neck is edged in white lace.

Pattern pieces required: Vest front/back 4X.
Cutting list: From winceyette cut two 4X.

Making up

• With right sides facing, stitch front and back together at shoulders using a run and fell seam (see page 9).

Anne of Green Gables is immensely popular in Japan. There is an Anne Academy, national fan clubs and a school of nursing, which is nicknamed The Green Gables School of Nursing and is sister school with the University of Prince Edward Island's School of Nursing.

collector's focus

- Turn neck edge in 6mm (¼in).
  Winceyette stretches when sewn,
  especially on the bias, so you need
  to use a gathering stitch and then
  pull the stitching up to reform the
  neck edge. Hand stitch lace edging
  all around the neck and pull out
  the original gathering stitches.
- Turn 6mm (¼in) in at the armholes
  using the gathering stitch. Pull up
  stitching to reform the armholes,
  this time leaving the stitching in.
  Tie a knot at each end of the
  stitching to retain the shape.
- With right sides facing, stitch sides
  together using a run and fell seam.
- Using a small, tight zigzag stitch,
  stitch around the bottom edge of
  the vest, pulling on the fabric as
  you sew to form a scalloped edge.

Anne's drawers

Made with an elasticized waist, the
only decoration on these drawers is
the scalloped edges to the legs.

Pattern pieces required: Drawers
front/back 4Y.
Cutting list: From winceyette cut
two 4Y (one reversed).

Making up

- Using a tight zigzag stitch form
  scalloped edges at the bottom of
  each leg as you did along the
  bottom edge of the vest.
- With right sides facing, stitch
  fronts and backs together at
  crotch, then stitch each leg
  together across crotch.
- Cut a length of 1cm (⅜in) elastic
  to fit doll's waist snugly. Stitch
  edge of elastic to edge of waistline
  using zigzag stitch and pulling up
  tightly as you sew. Turn the elastic
  down inside the drawers and stitch
  again along the same edge, still
  using a zigzag stitch and pulling
  up to fit drawers.

Diana's camisole

This camisole was made from an
antique modesty vest, however a
plain crêpe de chine or similar fabric
can be used. It has delicate ribbon
straps and fastens at the back.

Pattern pieces required: Camisole front/back 5P.

Cutting list: From crêpe de chine cut two 5P. If the silk has a patterned border, lay the top edge of the bodice front pattern piece against it before cutting out.

Making up

- With right sides facing, stitch the bodice front and back together at the sides using a run and fell seam (see page 9).
- Run a zigzag stitch around the armholes, the bottom edge and the back top edge. (If the front bodice is not cut from a patterned border, work as back top edge.) Turn the armhole edges in 3mm (⅛in) and hand stitch using tiny stitches. Turn the bottom and top back edges in 6mm (¼in) and stitch in the same way.
- Cut ribbon straps to fit the doll and hand stitch them to the inside upper front corners, turning under the ends. Sew snap fasteners to the inside upper back corners and to the remaining ends of the ribbon straps, turning under the ends.

Diana's bloomers

Tiny bows are stitched to the gathers just below the knee on these bloomers, which are made from fine cotton lawn. Under her bloomers Diana wears white stockings. See page 12 for instructions.

Pattern pieces required: Bloomers front/back 5Q.

Cutting list: From cotton lawn cut two 5Q (one reversed).

Making up

- Press up 6mm (¼in) at the bottom

of each leg. Turn up another 6mm (¼in) and stitch in place.

- Measure round the doll's leg just below the knee and mark the measurement on the 6mm (¼in) elastic. Stitch elastic to legs where indicated, using a zigzag stitch and pulling up on the elastic until the mark hits the other side. Trim off the end of the elastic and repeat for other leg.
- With right sides facing, stitch fronts and backs together at crotch, then each leg together across crotch. Finish the seam edges with a zigzag stitch to prevent fraying.
- Set 1cm (⅜in) elastic at the waist (see page 10).
- Tie two tiny bows using 3mm (⅛in) wide ribbon and hand stitch them to the front of each leg over the elastic.

Diana's half-petticoat

This petticoat has an elasticized waist with lace and ribbon trim.

Cutting list: From cotton lawn cut a rectangle 25cm (10in) long by 66cm (26in) wide.

Making up

- Turn up 6mm (¼in) at bottom edge of petticoat and stitch lace edging on wrong side over seam so that the lace hangs below the edge.
- With right sides facing, stitch sides together. Press seam open.
- Starting off-centre at the front, stitch ribbon trim over top edge of lace leaving about 13cm (5in) of loose ribbon at the start and finish to tie into a bow. Stitch the ribbon along both edges.
- Work an elasticized waistband (see page 10).

Rapunzel

In *Rapunzel*, one of the Brothers Grimm's most popular folktales, an evil enchantress imprisons Rapunzel in a tower with no door and uses her long braided hair as a ladder on which she climbs up to the window each day. A passing Prince hears Rapunzel singing and falls in love with her, and uses her hair to climb the tower, but on discovery the enchantress cuts off Rapunzel's braids and the Prince falls to the ground losing his sight. Rapunzel is turned out of the tower and her tears, falling on the Prince's eyes, restore his sight.

The Prince led Rapunzel to his kingdom where they lived happily ever after.

The doll shown is Monica, a German reproduction doll by C.M. Bergmann c.1916 from the author's collection. She is 51cm (20in) high.

The brothers Jacob and Wilhelm Grimm created what we know as *Grimm's Fairytales* in the early 1800s. They wanted to preserve Germanic folktales and they collected over 200 stories and ten children's legends, which included the familiar *Snow White, Sleeping Beauty, Cinderella, Hansel and Gretel, Rumpelstiltskin* and *The Musicians of Bremen*.

Rapunzel

'I will willingly go away with thee, but I do not know how to get down.'

This outfit fits a 51–56cm (20–22in) doll.

you will need

⅓ metre/yard polyester satin with 8 per cent elastic

30cm (12in) velveteen

30cm (12in) polyester satin lining

20cm (8in) metallic polyester or brocade

Lightweight iron-on interfacing

30cm (12in) of 6mm (¼in) wide lace trim

60 seed pearls

Flexi-lace or seam binding

Instructions

Gown

The empire waist bodice of Rapunzel's gown is dotted with seed pearls and edged in lace. It is lined and fastens at the back with snap fasteners. The long sleeves puff at the top and taper to a point over the back of the doll's hand. The skirt has a slight train.

Pattern pieces required: Bodice front 2I, Bodice back 2J, Upper sleeve 2K, Lower sleeve 2L, Sleeve facing 2M, Skirt front 2N, Skirt back 2P.
Cutting list: From metallic polyester cut two 2K. From velveteen cut one 2I and two 2J (one reversed). From satin lining fabric cut one 2I, and two 2J (one reversed). From polyester satin with elastic cut two 2L, two 2M, one 2N and one 2P.

Mix and match

If you are making up both Rapunzel and the Prince's outfits, choose several contrasting colours and interchange them in the two costumes. In this tableau the Prince's doublet is made from metallic polyester and the underside of this fabric is used for Rapunzel's puffed sleeves and cap. The fabric used for the Prince's cape is used for Rapunzel's bodice lining, and the fabric for her gown lines the Prince's cape. Let your imagination go and try different combinations.

Making up

- Following the pattern guideline for position, stitch seed pearls on the bodice front.
- With right sides facing, stitch bodice front to bodice backs at shoulders. Press seams open and repeat for lining.

Throughout the years *Grimm's Fairytales* have been illustrated by dozens of artists. Some of the more famous include Arthur Rackham, E.H. Wehnert, Mabel Lucie Attwell, Fritz Kredel and Maurice Sendak. First editions of the collection published before 1900 are very rare indeed.

- Tack edge of lace to the right side edge of the bodice neckline with the lace facing downwards. With right sides facing, stitch the lining to the bodice around the neckline sandwiching the lace, and down the backs. Turn bodice to right side. The lace will now stand up around the neckline.
- With the lining and bodice together, overcast the remaining raw edges. The bodice and lining are now worked as one unit.
- Overcast the top and bottom of the upper sleeves to prevent fraying. Run two rows of gathering stitches at the top and bottom of each sleeve where indicated.
- With right sides together, stitch sleeve facing to the bottom of lower sleeve. Trim. Do not turn facing into sleeve at this time.
- Pull up gathers at the bottom of upper sleeve and with right sides facing, stitch to top of lower sleeve, distributing gathers evenly between the indication marks.
- Pull up gathers at the top of upper sleeve and with right sides facing, set to bodice using Method 2 (see page 11), distributing gathers

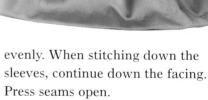

evenly. When stitching down the sleeves, continue down the facing. Press seams open.
- Turn facing up into sleeve, press and tack in place using tiny stitches about 12mm (½in) apart, which do not show on right side.

Fig 1

Fig 2

Pattern pieces required: Juliet cap 2Q.
Cutting list: From the metallic polyester cut one 2Q.
From the lining cut one 2Q.
Before cutting out, iron lightweight interfacing to both the cap and lining fabric.

Making up
- Transfer dart indication marks to wrong sides of cap and lining. Stitch darts starting at the outer edge with a small backstitch and tapering off at the tip without backstitching. Cut threads off about 12mm (½in) from tip. Press all darts in one direction.
- With right sides facing, stitch the cap and lining together leaving an opening just large enough to turn cap through to the right side. Press round the edges of the cap.
- Hand stitch decorative trim around the edge of the cap, tucking the raw ends in.

- To make the slash opening in the skirt, draw a 9cm (3½in) pencil line down the centre back skirt. Machine stitch close to and at either side of the line, tapering to nothing. Cut on pencil line between stitching.
- Turn back 6mm (¼in) on either side of the slash, tucking the edges in and hand stitch, tapering to nothing at the bottom. Fig 1.
- Overlap the left side with the right by a further 6mm (¼in) and secure at the bottom with a few small stitches. Fig 2.
- With right sides facing, stitch the front and back skirts together at the sides. Press seams open.

- Run two rows of gathering stitches at top of skirt and with right sides facing, stitch to bodice matching side seams and distributing gathers evenly.
- Stitch flexi-lace or seam binding to the bottom edge of skirt, turn up hem and hand stitch in place.
- Sew snap fasteners where indicated.

Juliet cap

This pretty Juliet cap is made from material that matches the upper sleeves of Rapunzel's gown. It is fully lined in satin polyester and trimmed round the edge with decorative gold braid.

Slippers

Rapunzel's slippers are made from velveteen with tiny seed pearls stitched to the tops to match the bodice of her gown.

Pattern pieces required: Slipper upper 3A, Slipper sole 3B.
Cutting list: From velveteen cut two 3A.
From polyester satin lining cut two 3A and two 3B (one reversed).

Iron medium weight interfacing to the satin soles before cutting out.

Making up

- Transfer seed pearl indication marks to the wrong side of each slipper upper and use to sew seed pearls on the right side.
- With right sides facing, stitch the upper and lining together around the top inner edge only. Trim and clip curves.
- Open lining out and with right sides facing, stitch across the back of upper and lining. Open out seam, turn upper down over lining and stay stitch all around the slipper, close to the edge.
- Run a gathering stitch by hand around the outer edge of the slipper upper, starting and finishing at the back seam. Pull up slightly to form a rounded toe.
- Turn upper wrong side out and tack to sole before stitching. Turn right side out.

did you know?

The name Rapunzel comes from *campanula rapunculus*, the Latin for turnip. During her pregnancy Rapunzel's mother craved turnips. She persuaded her husband to steal some from a neighbour's garden but the garden belonged to an enchantress, who caught him. She would only let him have the turnips if he gave her the baby when it was born. Afraid that his wife would die if her cravings weren't satisfied, he agreed to her demands.

The doll shown is a modern Elise doll and is from the author's collection. He stands 61cm (24in) high.

Prince

'Rapunzel, Rapunzel,
let down your hair, that I might
climb your golden stair.'

This outfit fits a 58–63cm (23–25in) doll.

you will need

¼ metre/yard cotton lawn

¼ metre/yard metallic polyester or brocade

⅓ metre/yard satin polyester

¼ metre/yard contrasting satin polyester
with 8 per cent elastic

2 metres/2⅛ yard of 12mm (½in) wide
decorative ribbon

12 small decorative shank buttons

51cm (20in) thin cording or ribbon

104cm (41in) gold braid trim

30cm (12in) square of suede

Shirring elastic

8 decorative buttons

1 hook and eye

1 button

4 snap fasteners

Feather

Instructions

Chemise

The chemise is made from four identical pieces of fabric that make up the front, back and sleeves. Elastic at the wrists and a drawstring at the neck pull it into shape.

Pattern pieces required: Chemise 2R and Chemise facing 2S.

Cutting list: From cotton lawn cut four 2R and four 2S.

Making up

- With right sides facing, stitch all four pieces together from A to B. Press seams open. Do the same with the facings, stitching together at the ends.
- Overcast the bottom edge of the facing and with right sides together, stitch the upper edge of the facing to the chemise at the neckline. Turn the facing over the chemise, press and stitch facing down along edge and again 12mm (½in) from edge, forming a casing.
- At the centre of one chemise section, snip a small opening on the right side between the two rows of stitches. Take care to only cut the front layer of fabric. Fig 1. Using a single strand of thread, work buttonhole stitch around the opening, again being careful not to catch the back layer of fabric. This section is now the front of the chemise. Using a bodkin or safety pin, run the cording or ribbon through one side of the opening round the neck and back out again. Put the chemise on the doll, pull up the cording and tie in a bow. Trim ends to reasonable length, but not so short that you lose them when the neck of the chemise is loosened.

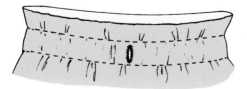

Fig 1

- The sections on either side of the front section now become the sleeves. Set shirring elastic to fit doll's wrist, 6cm (2½in) up from end of sleeve (see page 10).
- With right sides facing, stitch up the sides and down the sleeves. Press seams open and work a 3mm (⅛in) hem.
- At the bottom of the chemise work a 6mm (¼in) hem.

Doublet

Our Prince is a paragon of chivalry in his fully lined doublet of fine brocade that fastens down the back with four snap fasteners. Gold buttons decorate the front and epaulets adorn the shoulders.

Pattern pieces required: Doublet front 2U, Doublet back 2V, Epaulet 2W.
Cutting list: From metallic polyester cut one 2U, two 2V (one reversed) and four 2W.
From satin polyester cut one 2U and two 2V (one reversed).

Making up

- Stitch darts in the backs and press towards centre. Repeat for lining.
- With right sides facing, stitch doublet front and backs together at shoulders. Repeat for lining. Press seams open.
- With right sides facing, stitch two pairs of epaulets together down the outer curved edge. Turn, press and topstitch the two raw edges together close to the edge.
- With right sides facing, centre raw edge of epaulet to seam of shoulder at edge and tack in place.
- With right sides facing, stitch doublet and lining together around neck, down the backs and around armholes, sandwiching the epaulets. Stitch across the front and backs at the bottom to within 6mm (¼in) of the sides. Trim and notch seam allowances. Turn the

doublet through to the right side and press.

- With right sides facing, stitch the front and back of the doublet together at the sides, leaving the lining free. Turn the raw edges of the lining in and hand stitch the openings closed. Press.
- Work snap fasteners at the back where indicated and sew decorative buttons down the front.

Breeches

The breeches have waist and leg bands and lengths of ribbon stitched over the bloused shape to give the slashed effect that was popular in the 16th century.

Pattern pieces required: Breeches 2T.
Cutting list: From satin polyester cut four 2T, one waistband 6cm (2½in) by the doll's waistline plus 2.5cm (1in) and two leg bands 5cm (2in) by the doll's thigh at widest point plus 12mm (½in).

Making up
- Overlock or overcast all the raw edges of the breeches.
- With right sides facing, stitch two sections together at the sides.

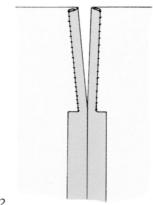

Fig 2

Repeat for other two sections. You now have two units.

- With right sides facing, stitch one unit to the other up the front on one side and only to the indication mark on the other side. Make a snip halfway into the seam allowance at the bottom of the opening, press seams open, turn raw edge of opening into snip and hand stitch in place. Fig 2.
- Cover the seams each side of the breeches by pinning lengths of decorative ribbon from the top to the bottom and then at regular intervals round the breeches. Stitch in place. Run two rows of gathering stitches at the waist and legs where indicated.
- With right sides facing, fold the waistband in half lengthwise and stitch together across each end. Turn to right side and press.

- Pin waistband to wrong side of waistline pulling up and distributing gathers evenly. Leave 12mm (½in) free at one end of waistband for overlap. Stitch then turn waistband over breeches, turn raw edge in and topstitch in place. Work buttonhole closure.
- Pull up gathering stitches at legs and with right sides facing, stitch leg bands to leg openings. Run zigzag stitching on raw edge of leg band. Fold breeches with right sides facing and stitch across the crotch and down the leg bands. Press seams open. Turn leg bands over legs, and tack in place. Turn breeches right side out and topstitch leg bands close to seam.

Cape

The cape is fully lined with a contrasting colour and is edged in gold trim. It has a wide collar and ties at the neck.

Pattern pieces required: Cape front 2X, Cape back 2Y, Collar 2Z.
Cutting list: From main satin polyester cut two 2X (one reversed), one 2Y and two 2Z.
From contrasting satin polyester cut two 2X (one reversed) and one 2Y. Press lightweight iron-on interfacing to the wrong side of one collar piece before cutting out.

Jacob and Wilhelm Grimm made major contributions in the fields of German mythology, legend, heroic sagas, essays, religion and law and they also embarked on the ambitious project of compiling the first German dictionary. In 1819 they both received honorary doctorates from the University of Marburg for their prolific work in linguistics, folklore and medieval legends.

Making up

- With right sides facing, stitch cape sides and back together matching notches. Repeat for lining. Press seams open.
- With right sides facing, stitch cape to lining leaving neck edge open. Trim, turn and press. Topstitch cape and lining together at neckline.
- Starting at one side of cape, topstitch braid trim all the way around except for the neck edge. Match the top thread on your machine to the colour of the trim and the bobbin thread to the colour of the lining, so the stitching blends in.
- With right sides facing, stitch collar pieces together leaving neck edge open. Clip corners, turn and press. The interfaced side is the underside of the collar.
- With right sides facing, stitch the underside of the collar to the cape at the neck. Turn the topside of the collar over the cape; tuck in raw edge and hand stitch in place.
- Stitch about 15cm (6in) of narrow gold cord to cape just under the collar for a tie.

Plumed beret

The Prince's beret is fully lined and is topped with a feather. It is set at a jaunty angle on the side of his head, with the feather swept back.

Cutting list: From contrasting satin polyester cut three circles 19cm (7½in) diameter. Cut out a 7.5cm (3in) diameter circle from the centre of two of the circles. This will be the underside of the beret. The full circle is the brim.

Making up

- With the wrong sides of the two undersides facing, stitch around the centre circle. Trim, turn to right side and press. Stitch the outer edges together.
- With the right side of the brim over the underside of beret, stitch around the outside edge. Trim, turn and press.
- Add a feather and small bow as shown.

Poulaine shoes

The poulaine shoes have turned down cuffs and long turned up pointed toes which are stuffed to keep their shape.

Pattern pieces required: Poulaine upper 3C, Poulaine cuff 3D, Poulaine sole 3E.

Cutting list: From suede cut four 3C (two reversed), four 3D (two reversed) and two 3E (one reversed).

Making up

- With right sides facing, stitch two uppers together from A to B and from C to D. Notch curves.
- With right sides facing, stitch upper to sole matching notches and keeping seams open. Trim seam and turn right side out.
- With right sides facing, stitch pairs of cuffs together at each side. Trim seams. Push cuff with right side out, into poulaine, matching notches, and stitch together around top edge. Trim and turn cuff over the top.
- Stuff polyester filling into the toes to hold them up in a nice curve.

In medieval days, only the aristocracy wore the poulaine shoe. The length of the point denoted their wealth – the more land they owned, the longer the point. The toes were stuffed with straw or cotton to hold them up. Later, a limit was placed on the length of the toe you could wear.

What's underneath?

Rapunzel's underwear consists of a full-length organza petticoat over pantalets. The bodice of the petticoat has a cotton lawn lining and the neckline has a decorative trim binding. The long pantalets have decorative trims around the ankles. The Prince wears hose in a rich shade of purple. If you are dying the fabric, dye it before the hose are made up.

you will need

⅓ metre/yard organza

¼ metre/yard white cotton lawn

Lightweight iron-on interfacing

Flexi-lace or seam binding to match organza

Small amount of decorative trim and trim binding

2 snap fasteners

1cm (⅜in) wide flat elastic

Stretchable cotton fabric (amount determined by length of hose cut on the straight of the fabric) or a pair of children's hose cut down.

Instructions

Rapunzel's petticoat

A floating organza skirt stitched to an organza-covered bodice makes a dainty petticoat.

Pattern pieces required: Bodice front 3F and Bodice back 3G.

Cutting list: From organza cut one 3F and two 3G (one reversed), one skirt front 30cm (12in) wide by 38cm (15in) long and one skirt back 76cm (30in) wide by 38cm (15in) long.

From cotton lawn cut one 3F and two 3G (one reversed).
Press lightweight iron-on interfacing to one bodice front piece and one pair of bodice backs before cutting out the pieces.

Making up

- With right sides facing, stitch bodice front and backs together at the shoulders. Repeat for bodice lining. Trim and press seams towards the back.
- With right sides facing, stitch the bodice and lining together around the armholes and at the backs. Turn to right side and press.
- Run a zigzag stitch around the neck edge to hold the bodice and lining together. Bind the raw edges with decorative trim binding.
- Open out the bodice from the lining under the armhole and with right sides facing, stitch front to backs. Press seams open, turn to right side and press again.
- With right sides facing, stitch the front and back skirts together at both sides using a run and fell seam (see page 9).
- Work a 7.5cm (3in) slash opening at the centre back (see page 68, Fig 1 and Fig 2).
- Run two rows of gathering stitches at the top of the skirt and with right sides facing, pin skirt to bodice matching side seams and adjusting gathers with most of the fullness at the back, and stitch in place leaving the lining free. Turn the raw edge of the bodice lining up, then over the skirt and hand stitch in place.
- Stitch flexi-lace seam binding to the skirt edge, turn hem up and hand stitch with small stitches.

- Work snap fasteners at the back where indicated.

Rapunzel's pantalets

The pantalets are made in the same way as Alice's drawers with the legs extended to ankle length.

Pattern pieces required: Pantalets front/back 3H.
Cutting list: From cotton lawn cut two 3H.

Making up

Work as for Alice's drawers (see page 25).

Prince's hose

To achieve exactly the right shade of purple the fabric was dyed before cutting out. Choose the dye suitable for synthetic or natural fibres depending on the fabric you are using to make them.

Pattern pieces required: Hose 3I.
Cutting list: Cut two 3I (one reversed).

Making up

- With right sides facing, stitch down each leg. Trim.
- Turn one leg right side out and push it down into the other leg and stitch around the crotch. Turn hose right side out.
- Cut a length of flat elastic to fit your doll's waistline. Stitch the ends of the elastic together forming a loop. Pin the loop to the top edge of the hose at the front, back and sides, using four pins. Now zigzag stitch the elastic to the hose pulling it up to fit the waistline as you stitch. (See sewing flat elastic under shirring elastic, page 10.)

did you know?

The Brothers Grimm were German, so most of the stories, with few exceptions, that had Princes in them, meant that the Prince was a nobleman, not the son of a monarch.

Pattern index

Patterns

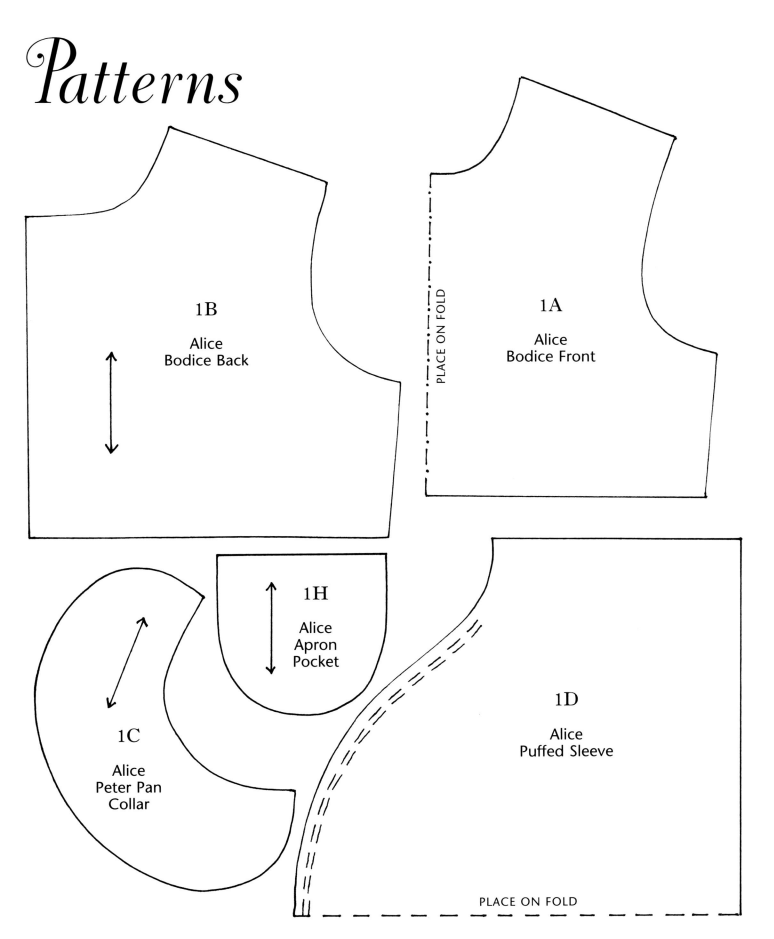

1B

Alice
Bodice Back

1A

Alice
Bodice Front

PLACE ON FOLD

1H

Alice
Apron
Pocket

1C

Alice
Peter Pan
Collar

1D

Alice
Puffed Sleeve

PLACE ON FOLD

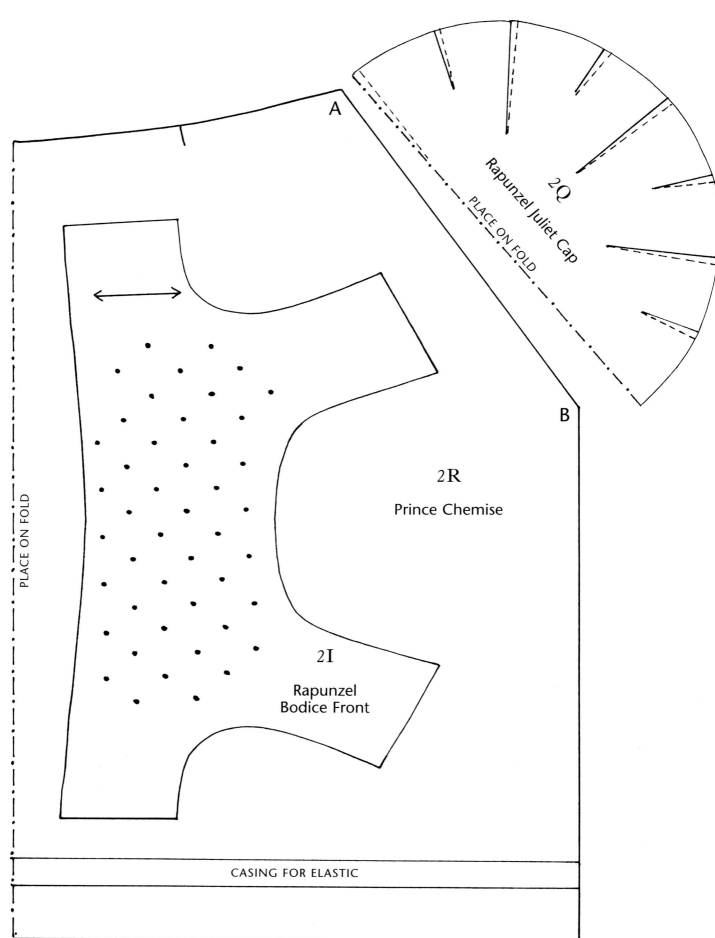

A

Rapunzel Juliet Cap

2Q

PLACE ON FOLD

B

PLACE ON FOLD

2R

Prince Chemise

2I

Rapunzel
Bodice Front

CASING FOR ELASTIC

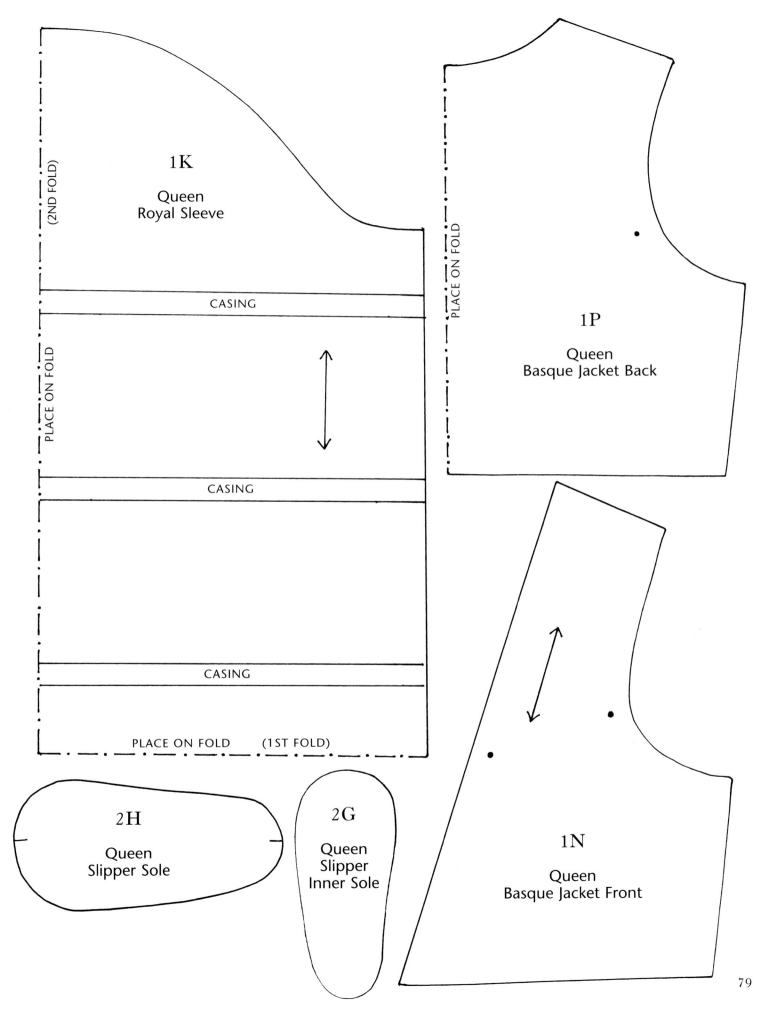

1K

Queen
Royal Sleeve

(2ND FOLD)

PLACE ON FOLD

CASING

CASING

CASING

PLACE ON FOLD   (1ST FOLD)

2H

Queen
Slipper Sole

2G

Queen
Slipper
Inner Sole

PLACE ON FOLD

1P

Queen
Basque Jacket Back

1N

Queen
Basque Jacket Front

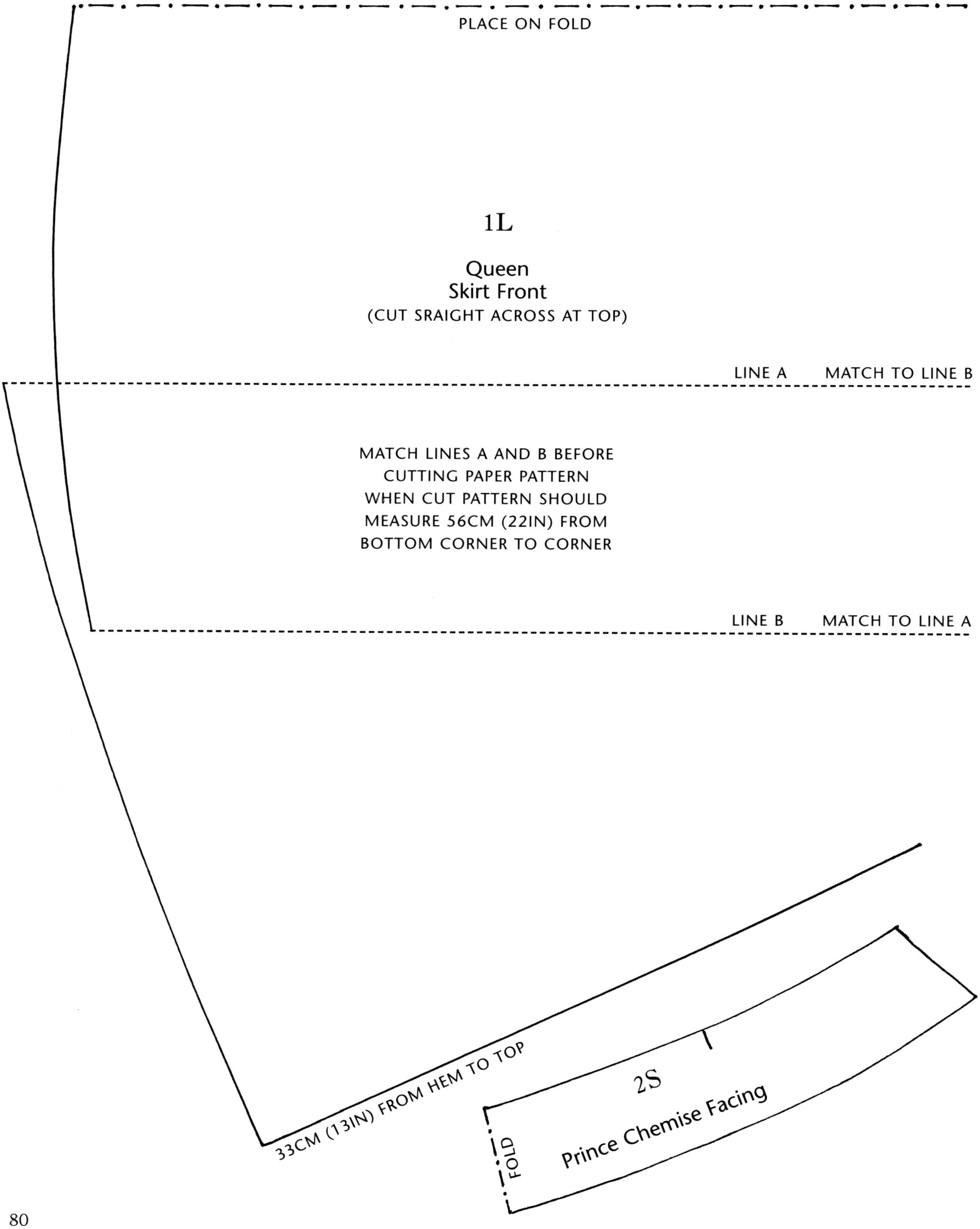

PLACE ON FOLD

1L

Queen
Skirt Front
(CUT SRAIGHT ACROSS AT TOP)

LINE A   MATCH TO LINE B

MATCH LINES A AND B BEFORE
CUTTING PAPER PATTERN
WHEN CUT PATTERN SHOULD
MEASURE 56CM (22IN) FROM
BOTTOM CORNER TO CORNER

LINE B   MATCH TO LINE A

33CM (13IN) FROM HEM TO TOP

2S
Prince Chemise Facing

FOLD

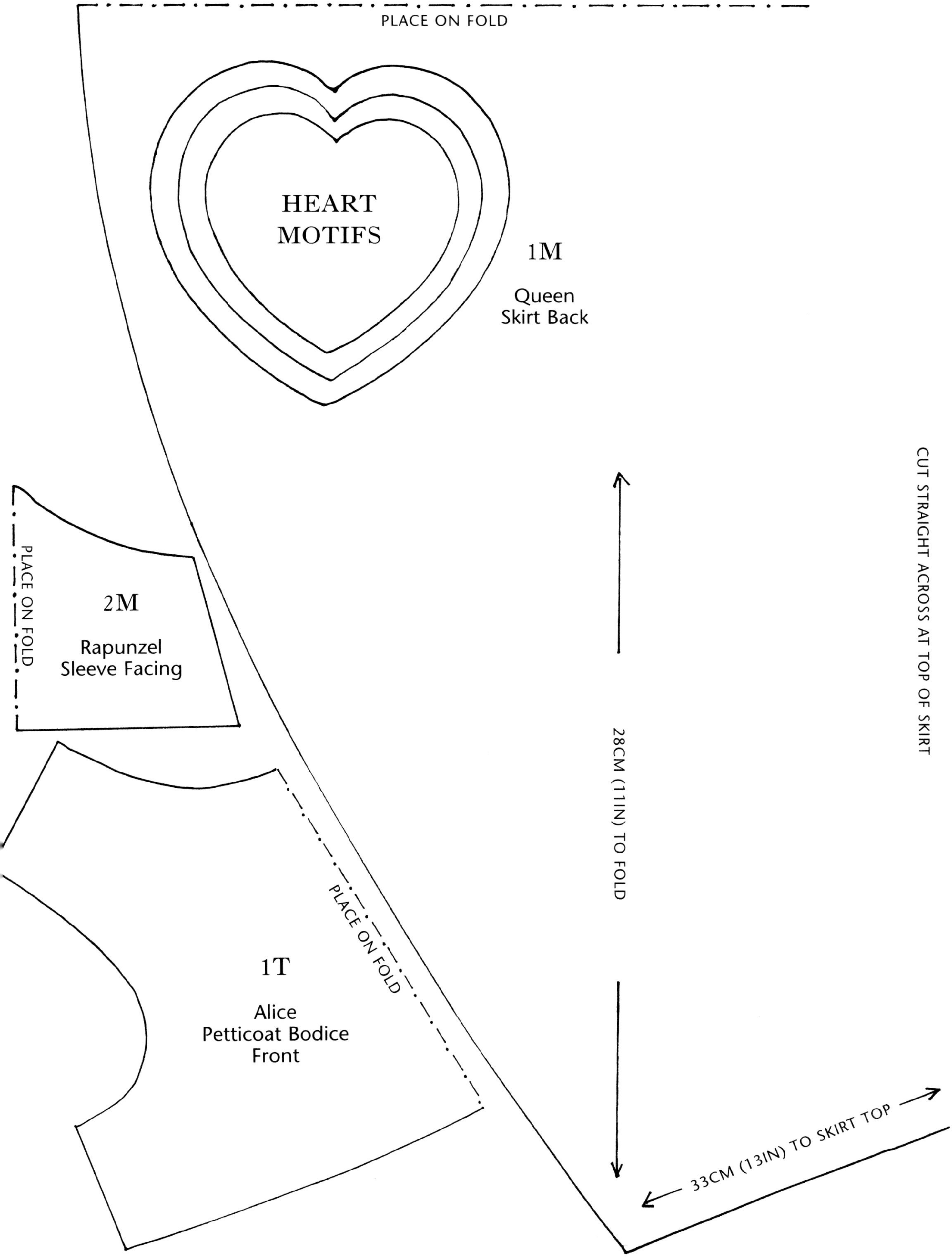

HEART
MOTIFS

1M

Queen
Skirt Back

2M

Rapunzel
Sleeve Facing

PLACE ON FOLD

PLACE ON FOLD

1T

Alice
Petticoat Bodice
Front

28CM (11IN) TO FOLD

CUT STRAIGHT ACROSS AT TOP OF SKIRT

33CM (13IN) TO SKIRT TOP

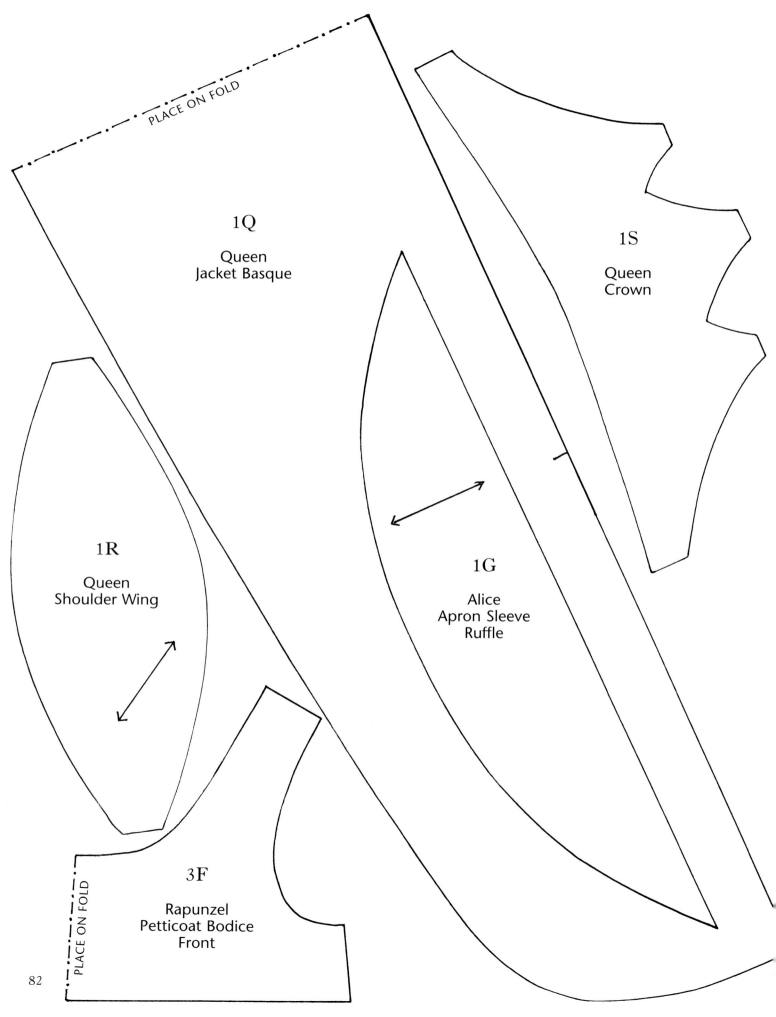

PLACE ON FOLD

1Q

Queen
Jacket Basque

1S

Queen
Crown

1R

Queen
Shoulder Wing

1G

Alice
Apron Sleeve
Ruffle

PLACE ON FOLD

3F

Rapunzel
Petticoat Bodice
Front

82

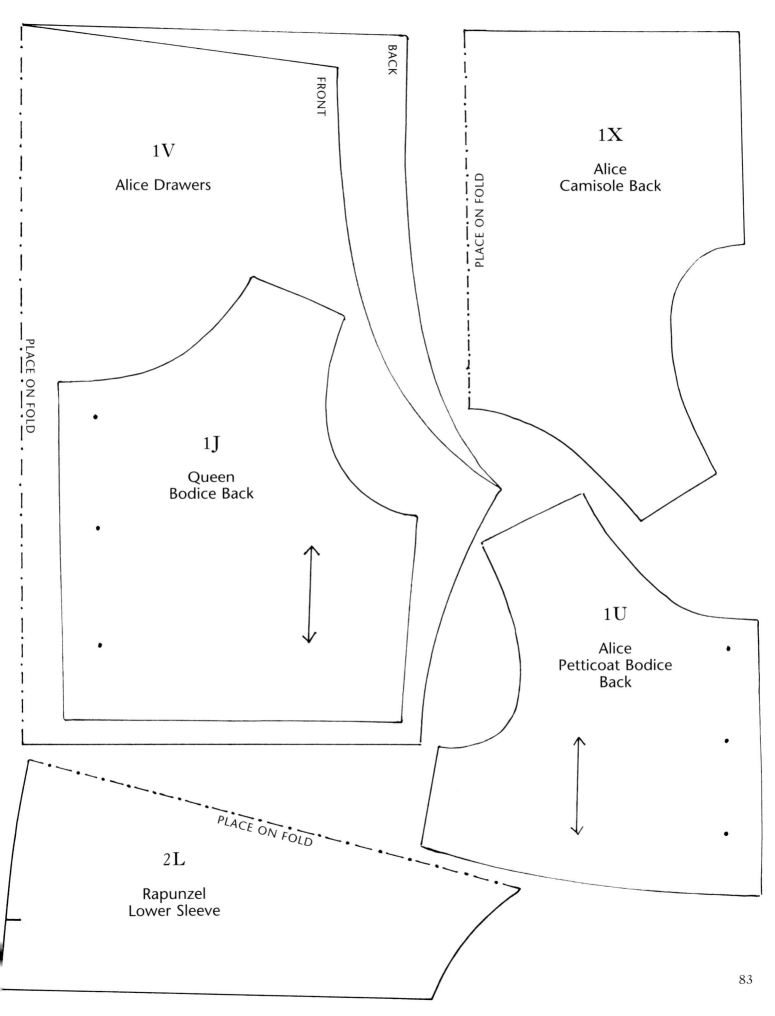

1V

Alice Drawers

BACK

FRONT

PLACE ON FOLD

1X

Alice
Camisole Back

PLACE ON FOLD

1J

Queen
Bodice Back

PLACE ON FOLD

1U

Alice
Petticoat Bodice
Back

PLACE ON FOLD

2L

Rapunzel
Lower Sleeve

83

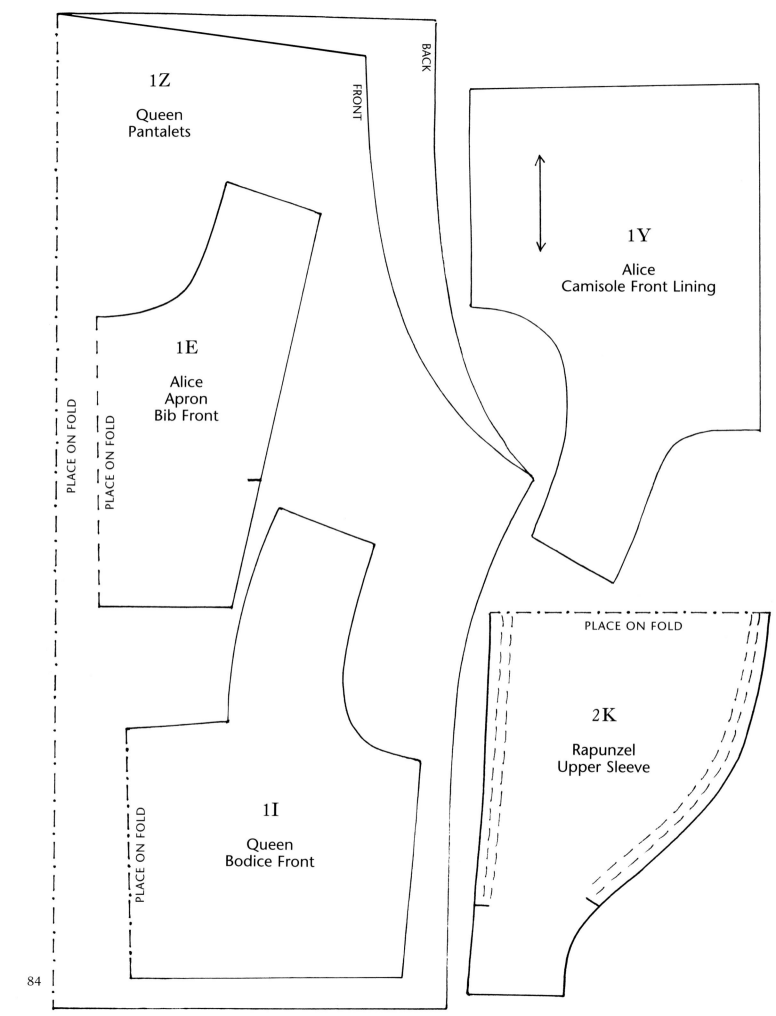

1Z

Queen
Pantalets

BACK

FRONT

1E

Alice
Apron
Bib Front

PLACE ON FOLD

PLACE ON FOLD

1I

Queen
Bodice Front

PLACE ON FOLD

PLACE ON FOLD

1Y

Alice
Camisole Front Lining

PLACE ON FOLD

2K

Rapunzel
Upper Sleeve

84

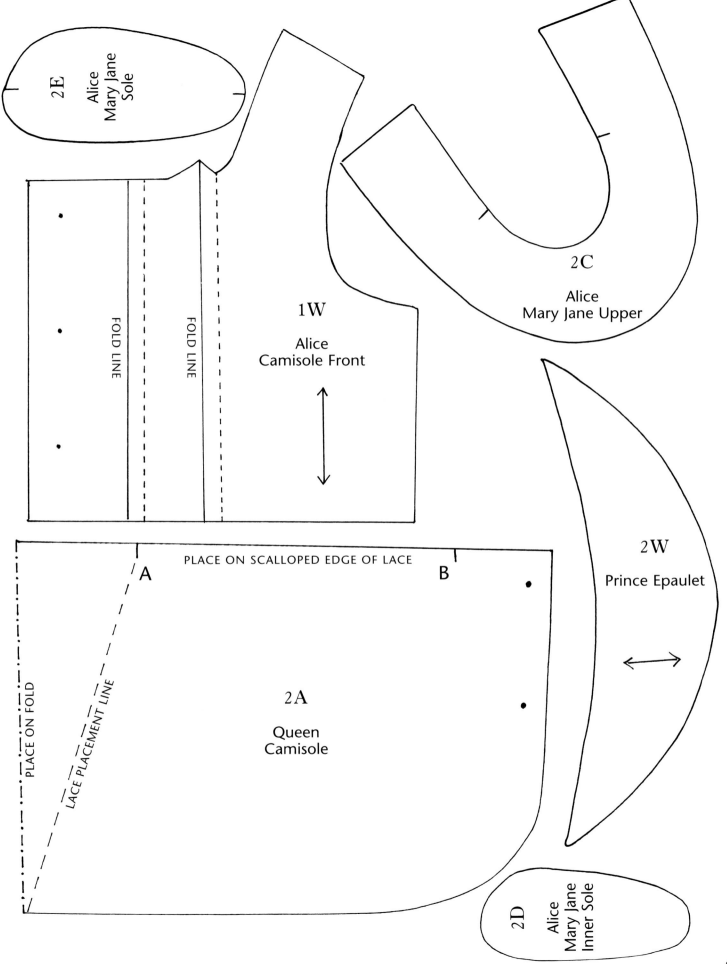

2E
Alice
Mary Jane
Sole

1W
Alice
Camisole Front

FOLD LINE

FOLD LINE

2C
Alice
Mary Jane Upper

PLACE ON SCALLOPED EDGE OF LACE

A

B

2A

Queen
Camisole

PLACE ON FOLD

LACE PLACEMENT LINE

2W
Prince Epaulet

2D
Alice
Mary Jane
Inner Sole

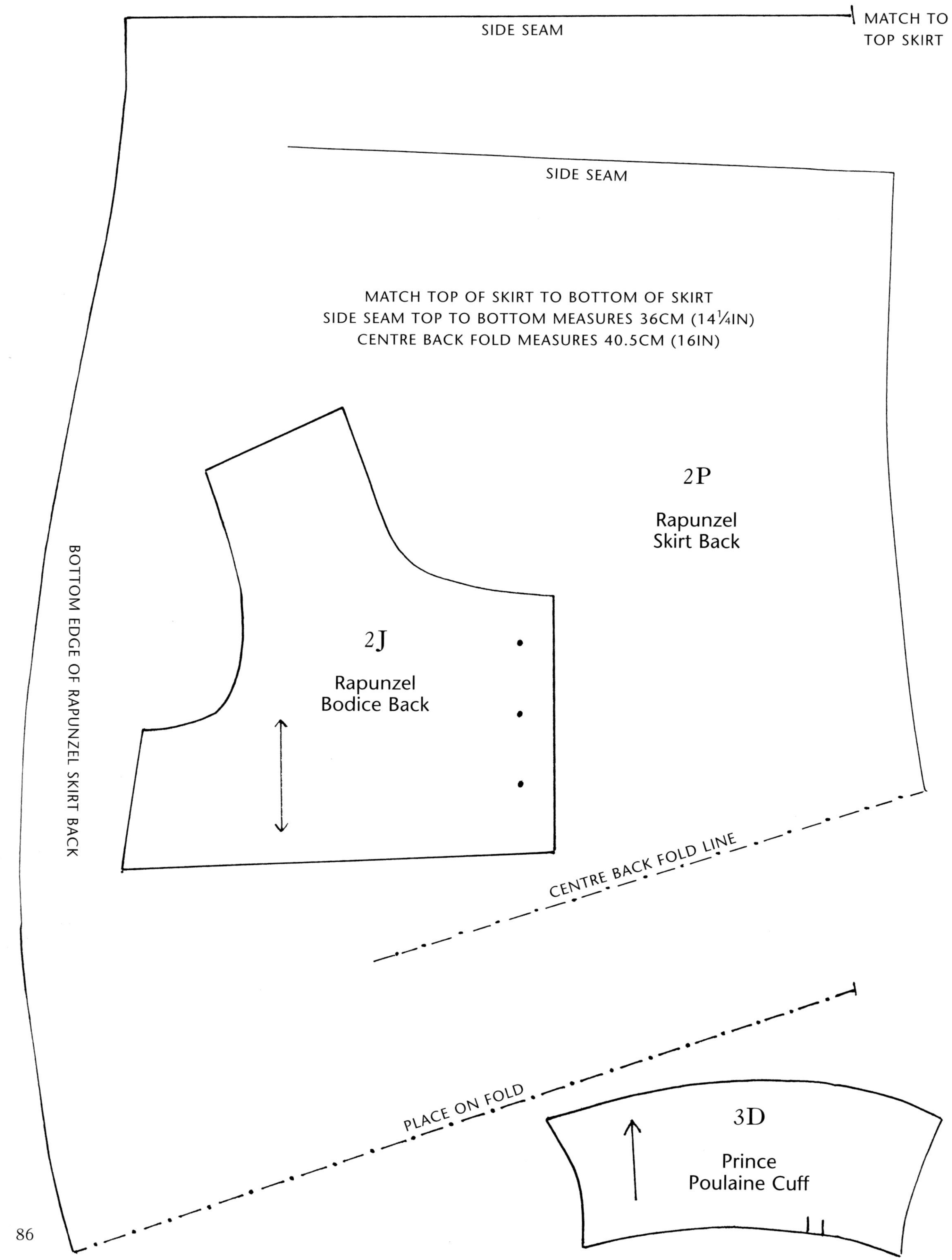

SIDE SEAM

MATCH TO
TOP SKIRT

SIDE SEAM

MATCH TOP OF SKIRT TO BOTTOM OF SKIRT
SIDE SEAM TOP TO BOTTOM MEASURES 36CM (14¼IN)
CENTRE BACK FOLD MEASURES 40.5CM (16IN)

2P

Rapunzel
Skirt Back

2J

Rapunzel
Bodice Back

BOTTOM EDGE OF RAPUNZEL SKIRT BACK

CENTRE BACK FOLD LINE

PLACE ON FOLD

3D

Prince
Poulaine Cuff

86

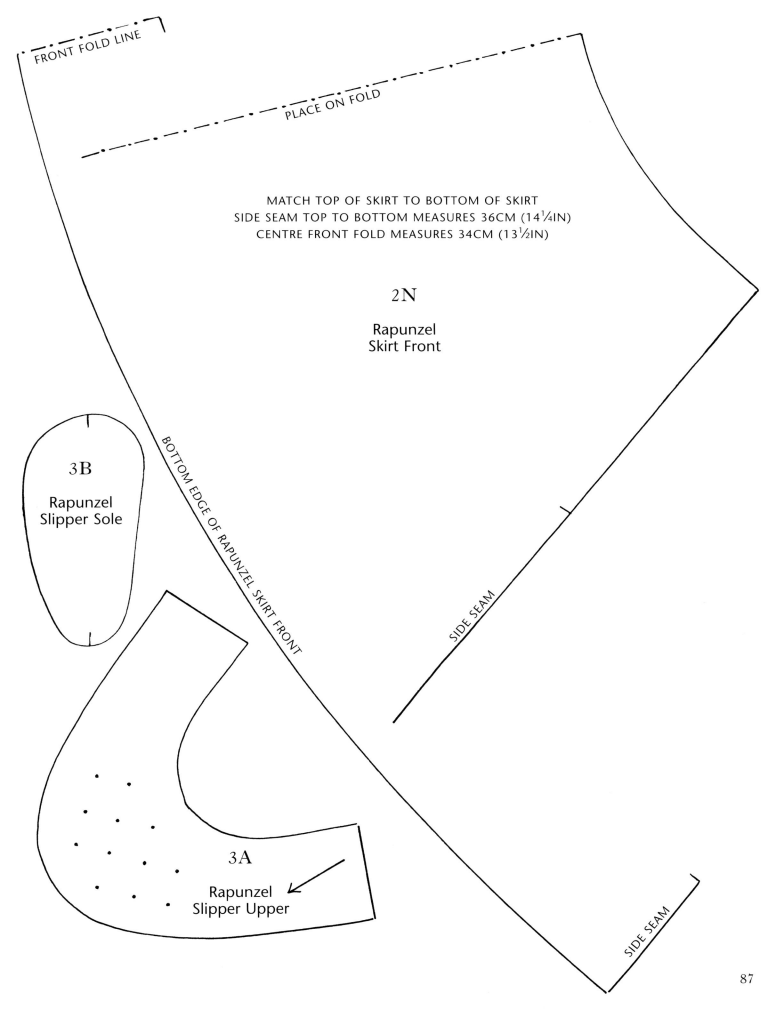

FRONT FOLD LINE

PLACE ON FOLD

MATCH TOP OF SKIRT TO BOTTOM OF SKIRT
SIDE SEAM TOP TO BOTTOM MEASURES 36CM (14¼IN)
CENTRE FRONT FOLD MEASURES 34CM (13½IN)

2N

Rapunzel
Skirt Front

3B

Rapunzel
Slipper Sole

BOTTOM EDGE OF RAPUNZEL SKIRT FRONT

SIDE SEAM

3A

Rapunzel
Slipper Upper

SIDE SEAM

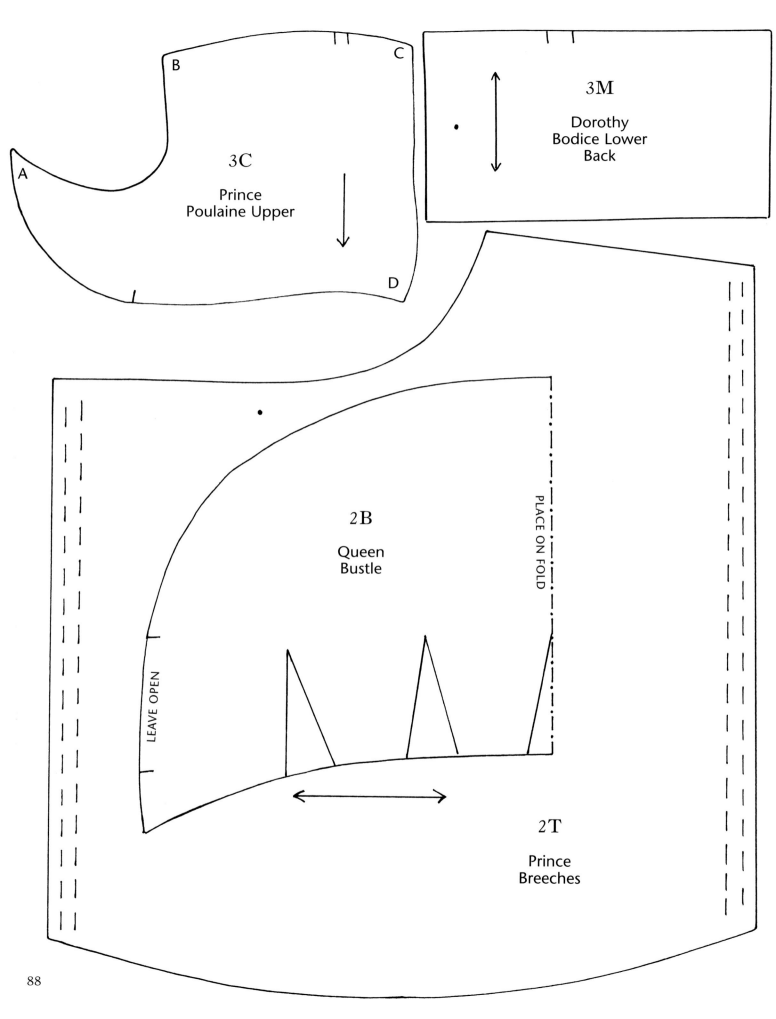

3C

Prince
Poulaine Upper

B

C

A

D

3M

Dorothy
Bodice Lower
Back

2B

Queen
Bustle

PLACE ON FOLD

LEAVE OPEN

2T

Prince
Breeches

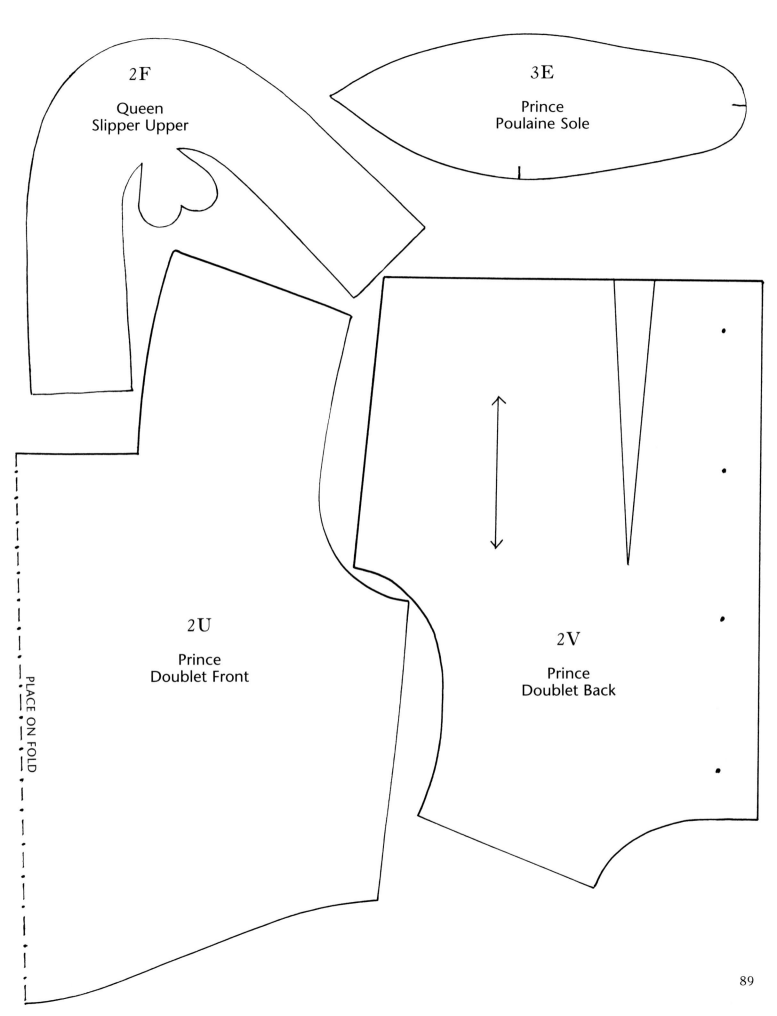

2F

Queen
Slipper Upper

3E

Prince
Poulaine Sole

2U

Prince
Doublet Front

2V

Prince
Doublet Back

PLACE ON FOLD

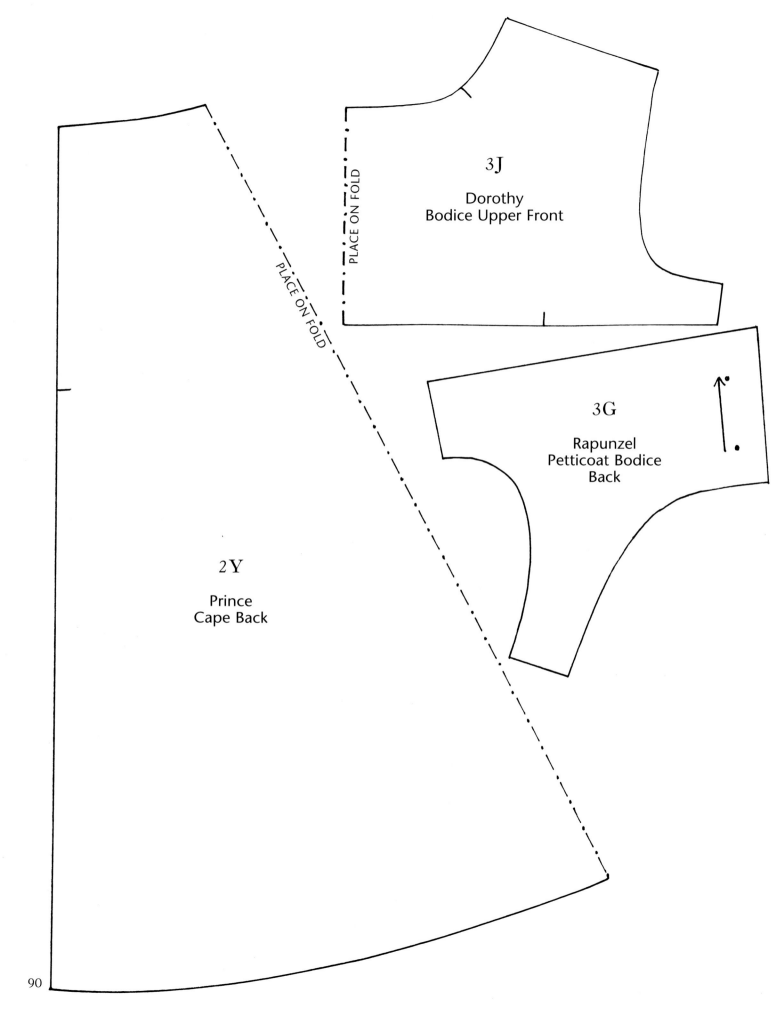

3J

Dorothy
Bodice Upper Front

PLACE ON FOLD

PLACE ON FOLD

3G

Rapunzel
Petticoat Bodice
Back

2Y

Prince
Cape Back

5G

Anne
Carpetbag End

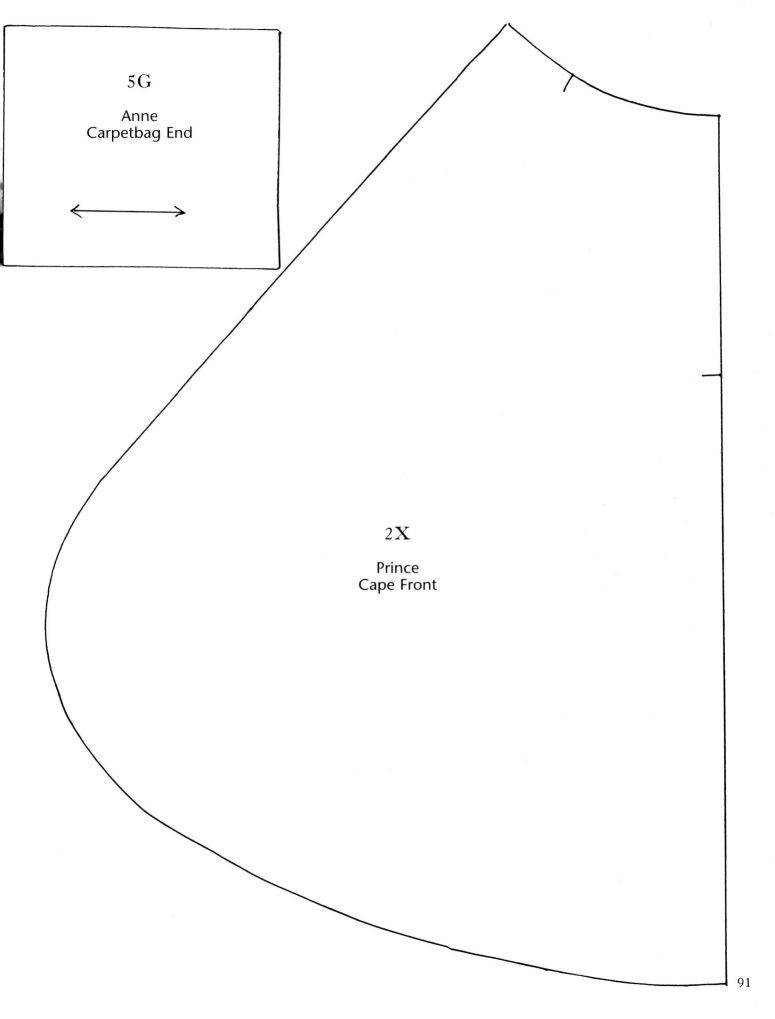

2X

Prince
Cape Front

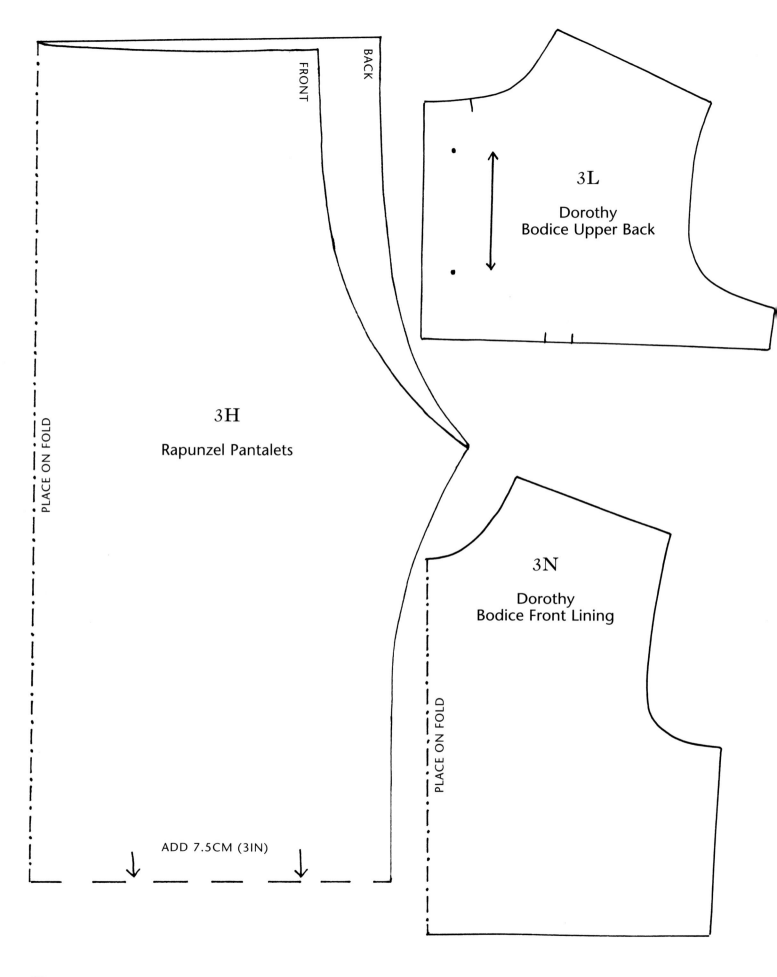

FRONT

BACK

PLACE ON FOLD

3H

Rapunzel Pantalets

ADD 7.5CM (3IN)

3L

Dorothy
Bodice Upper Back

3N

Dorothy
Bodice Front Lining

PLACE ON FOLD

92

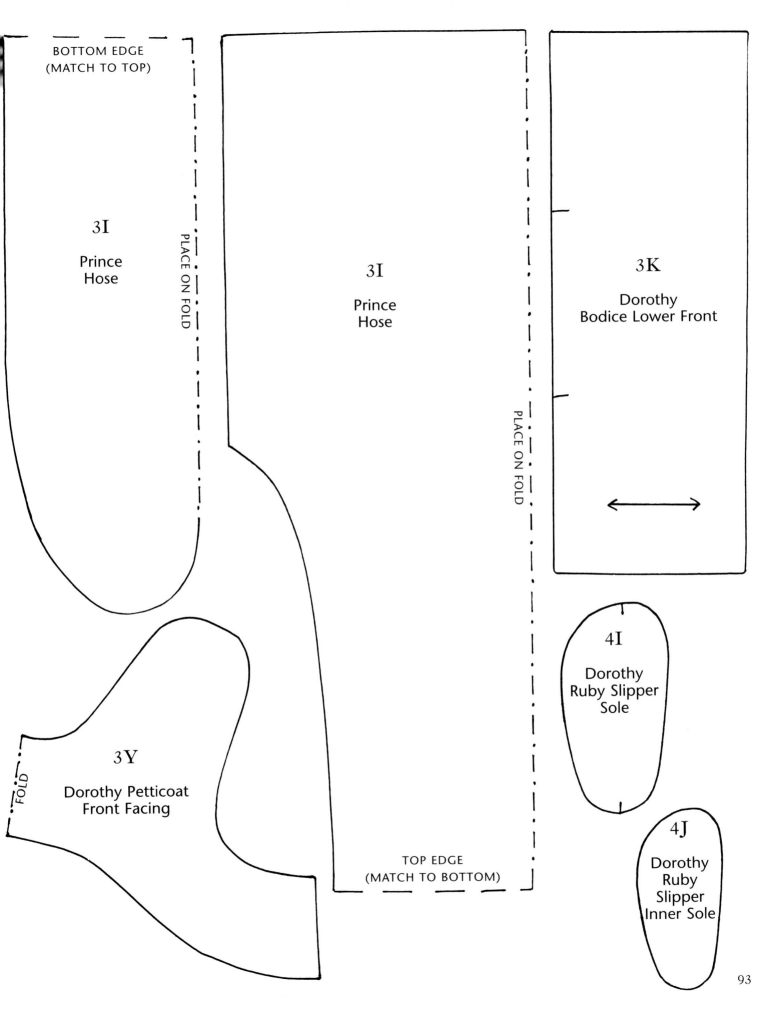

BOTTOM EDGE
(MATCH TO TOP)

3I

Prince
Hose

PLACE ON FOLD

3I

Prince
Hose

PLACE ON FOLD

3K

Dorothy
Bodice Lower Front

←——————→

FOLD

3Y

Dorothy Petticoat
Front Facing

TOP EDGE
(MATCH TO BOTTOM)

4I

Dorothy
Ruby Slipper
Sole

4J

Dorothy
Ruby
Slipper
Inner Sole

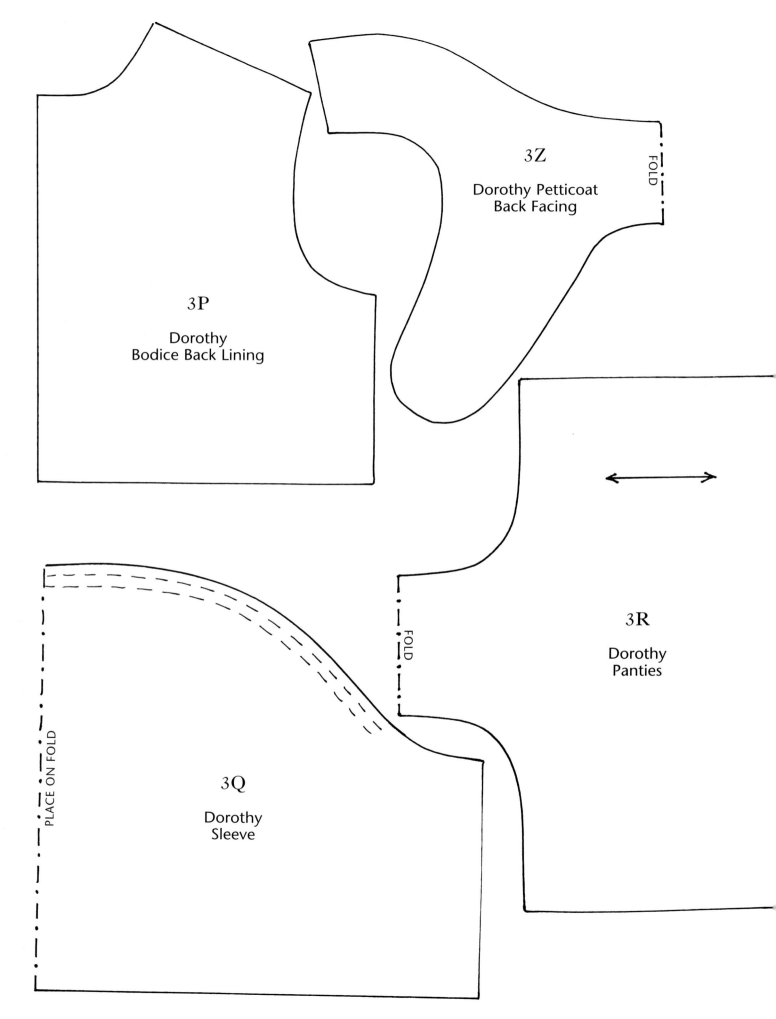

3Z

Dorothy Petticoat
Back Facing

FOLD

3P

Dorothy
Bodice Back Lining

3R

Dorothy
Panties

FOLD

PLACE ON FOLD

3Q

Dorothy
Sleeve

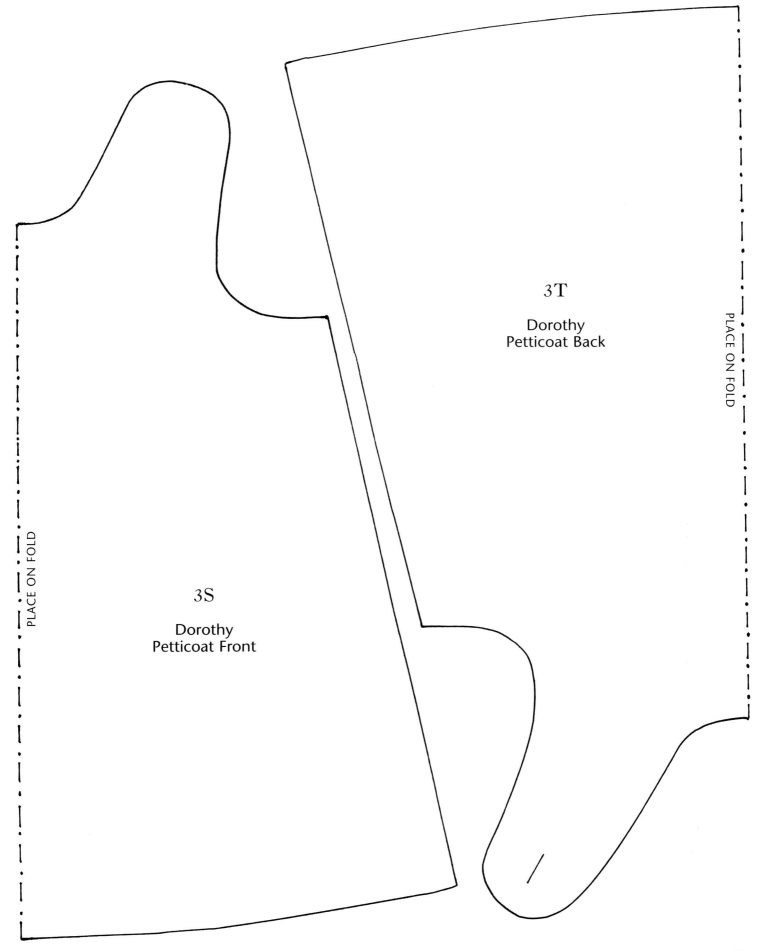

PLACE ON FOLD

3T

Dorothy
Petticoat Back

PLACE ON FOLD

PLACE ON FOLD

3S

Dorothy
Petticoat Front

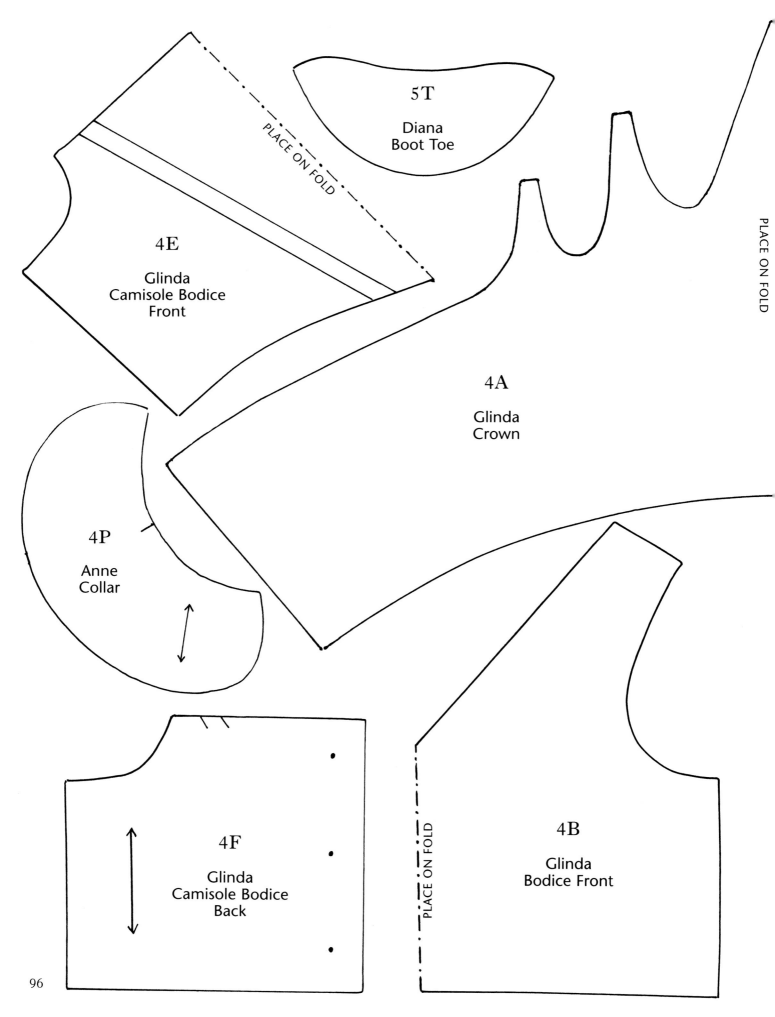

5T

Diana
Boot Toe

4E

Glinda
Camisole Bodice
Front

PLACE ON FOLD

PLACE ON FOLD

4A

Glinda
Crown

4P

Anne
Collar

4F

Glinda
Camisole Bodice
Back

PLACE ON FOLD

4B

Glinda
Bodice Front

96

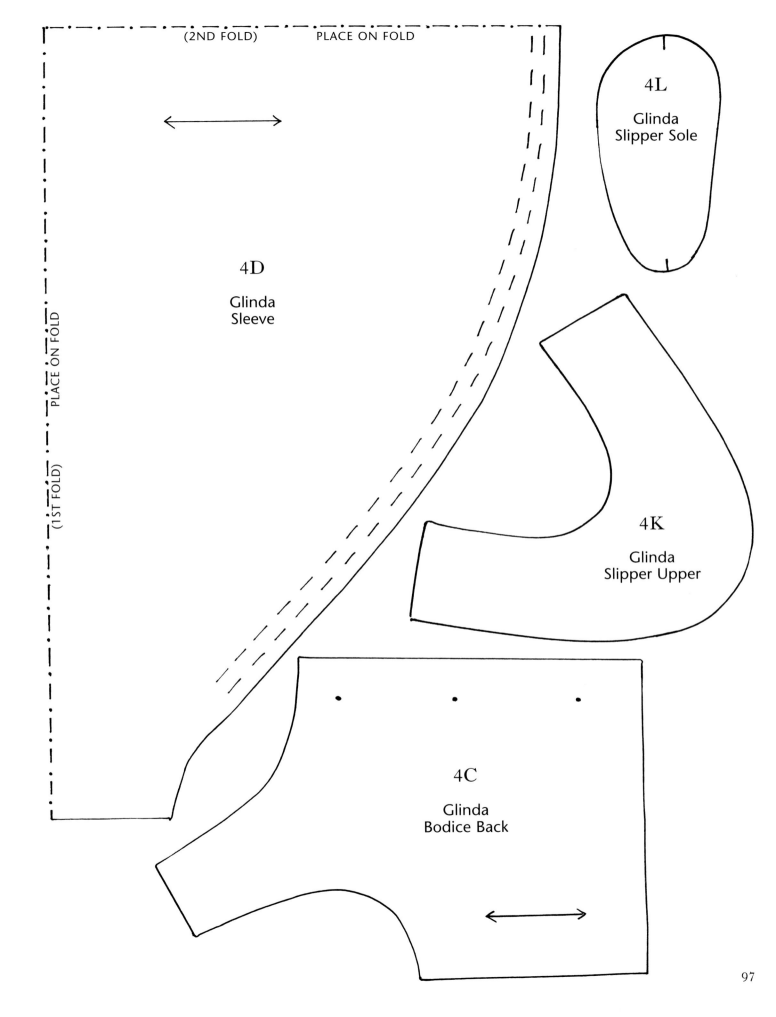

(2ND FOLD)   PLACE ON FOLD

PLACE ON FOLD

(1ST FOLD)

4D

Glinda
Sleeve

4L

Glinda
Slipper Sole

4K

Glinda
Slipper Upper

4C

Glinda
Bodice Back

97

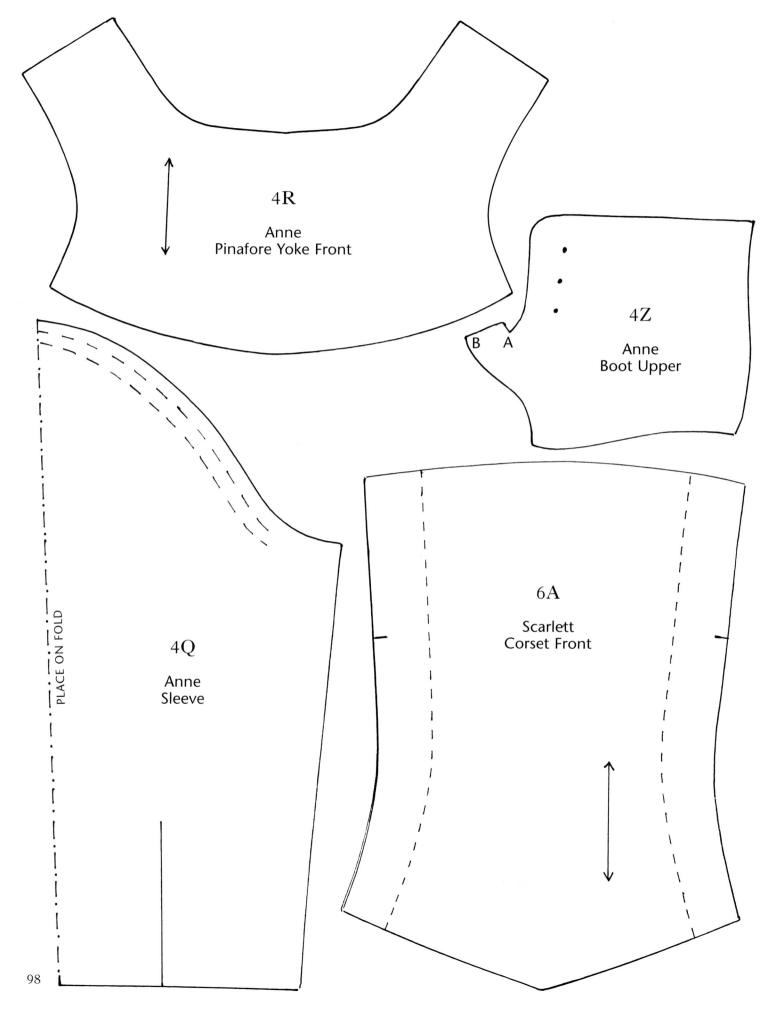

4R

Anne
Pinafore Yoke Front

4Z

Anne
Boot Upper

B   A

PLACE ON FOLD

4Q

Anne
Sleeve

6A

Scarlett
Corset Front

98

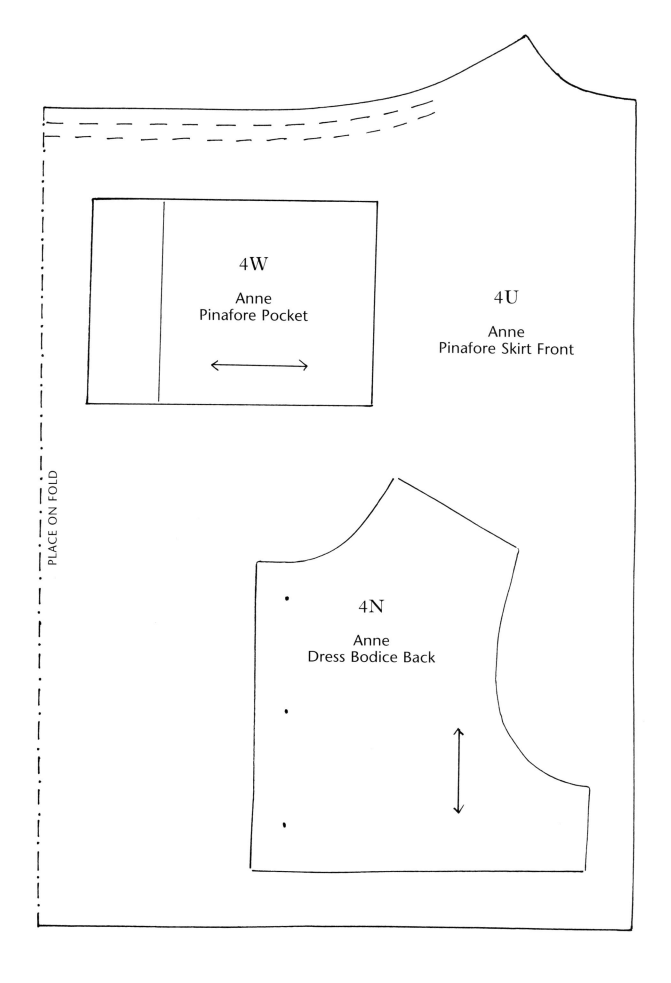

4W

Anne
Pinafore Pocket

4U

Anne
Pinafore Skirt Front

4N

Anne
Dress Bodice Back

PLACE ON FOLD

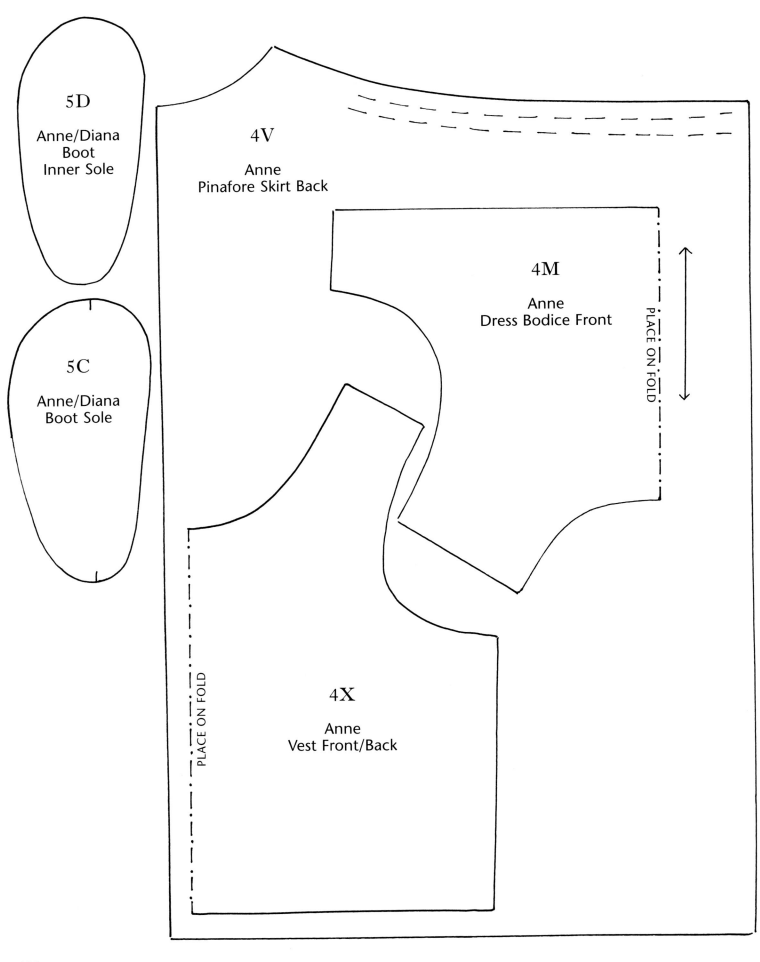

5D

Anne/Diana
Boot
Inner Sole

4V

Anne
Pinafore Skirt Back

4M

Anne
Dress Bodice Front

PLACE ON FOLD

5C

Anne/Diana
Boot Sole

PLACE ON FOLD

4X

Anne
Vest Front/Back

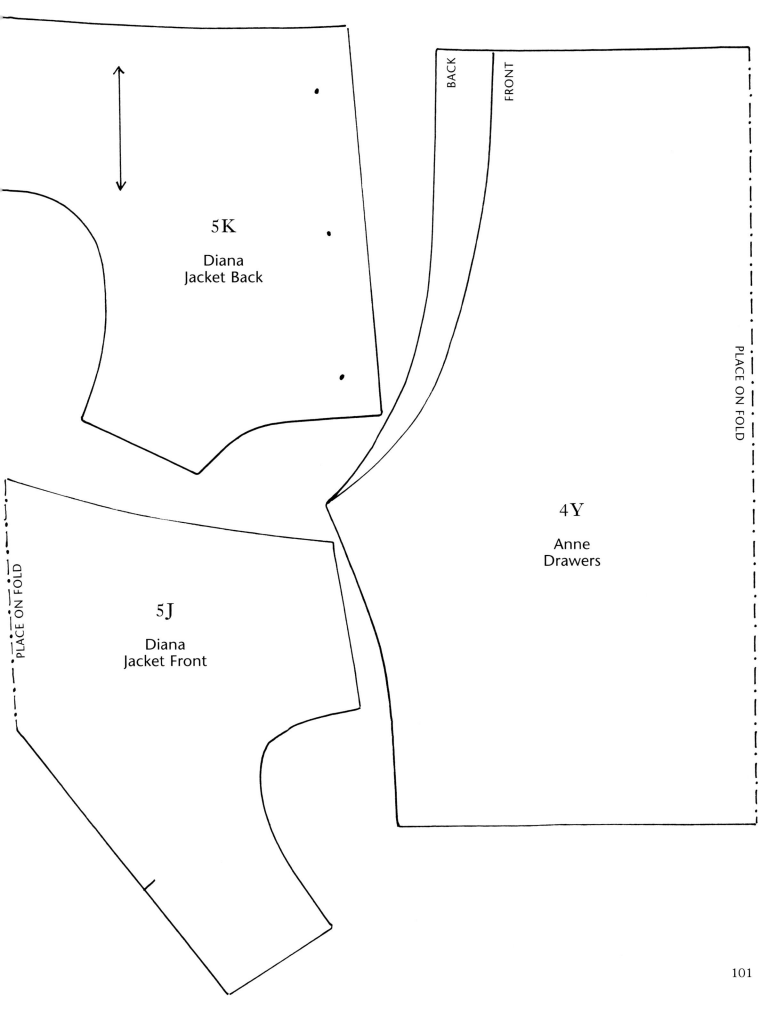

5K

Diana
Jacket Back

5J

Diana
Jacket Front

PLACE ON FOLD

BACK

FRONT

4Y

Anne
Drawers

PLACE ON FOLD

101

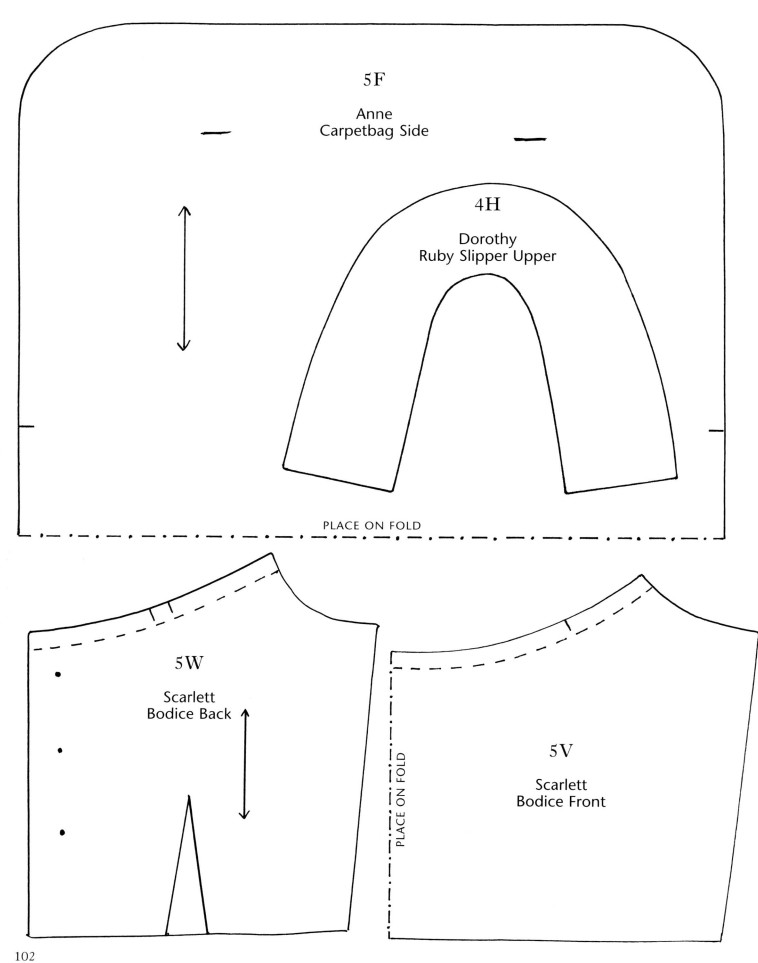

5F

Anne
Carpetbag Side

4H

Dorothy
Ruby Slipper Upper

PLACE ON FOLD

5W

Scarlett
Bodice Back

PLACE ON FOLD

5V

Scarlett
Bodice Front

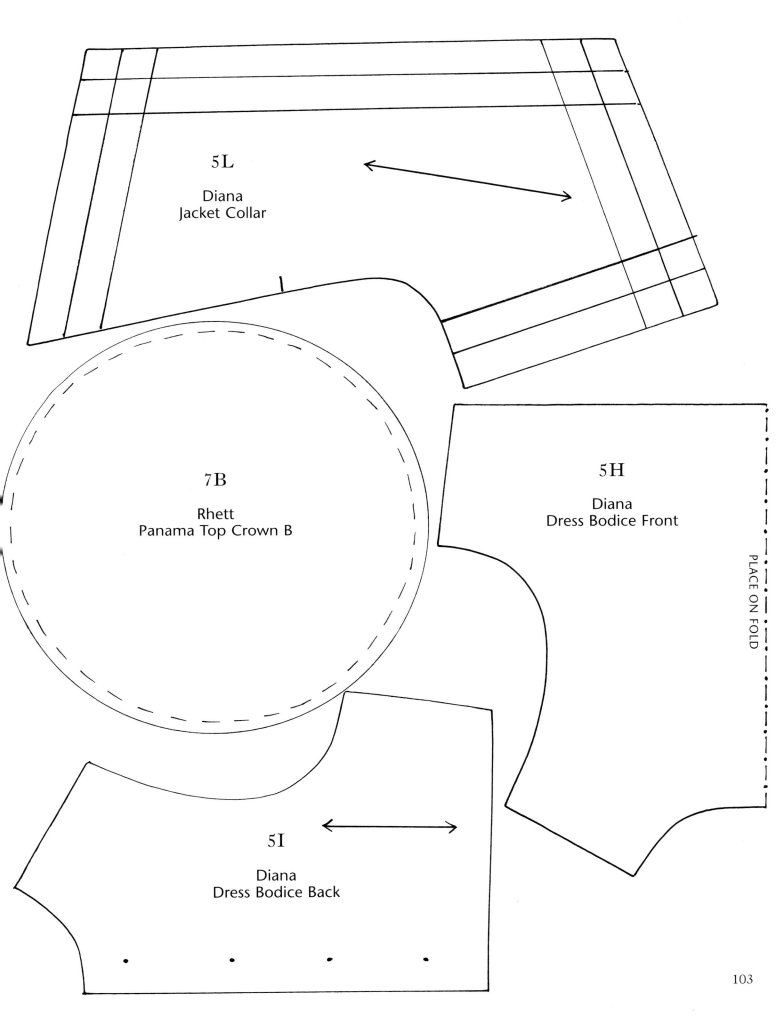

5L

Diana
Jacket Collar

7B

Rhett
Panama Top Crown B

5H

Diana
Dress Bodice Front

PLACE ON FOLD

5I

Diana
Dress Bodice Back

103

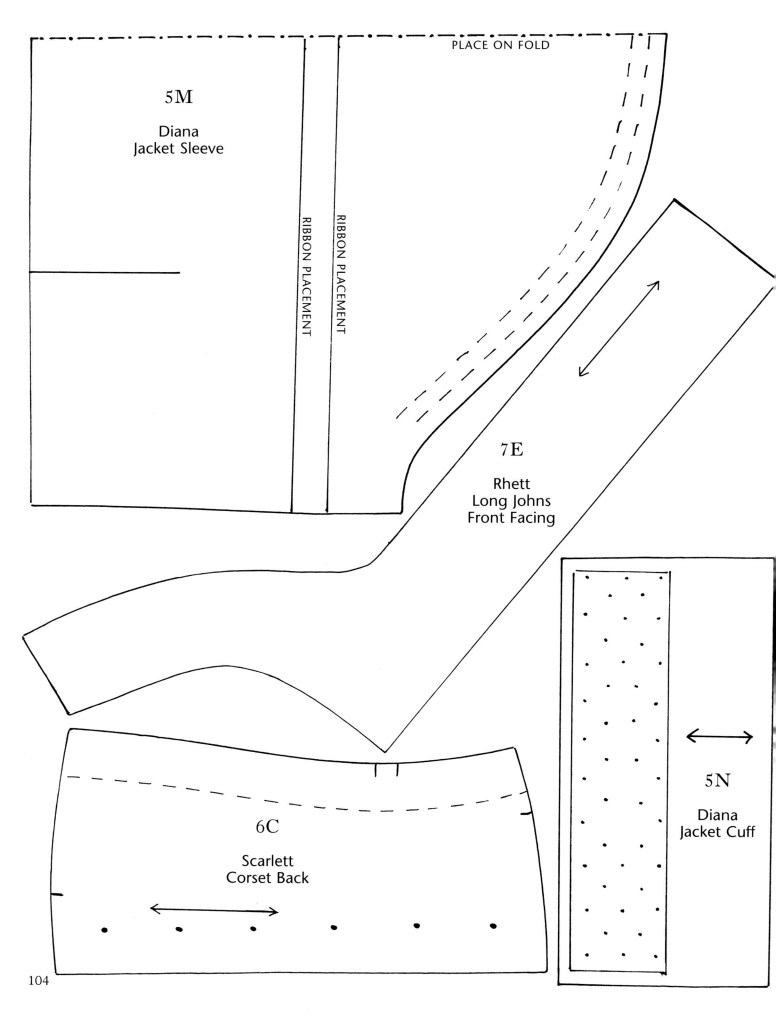

5M

Diana
Jacket Sleeve

PLACE ON FOLD

RIBBON PLACEMENT

RIBBON PLACEMENT

7E

Rhett
Long Johns
Front Facing

6C

Scarlett
Corset Back

5N

Diana
Jacket Cuff

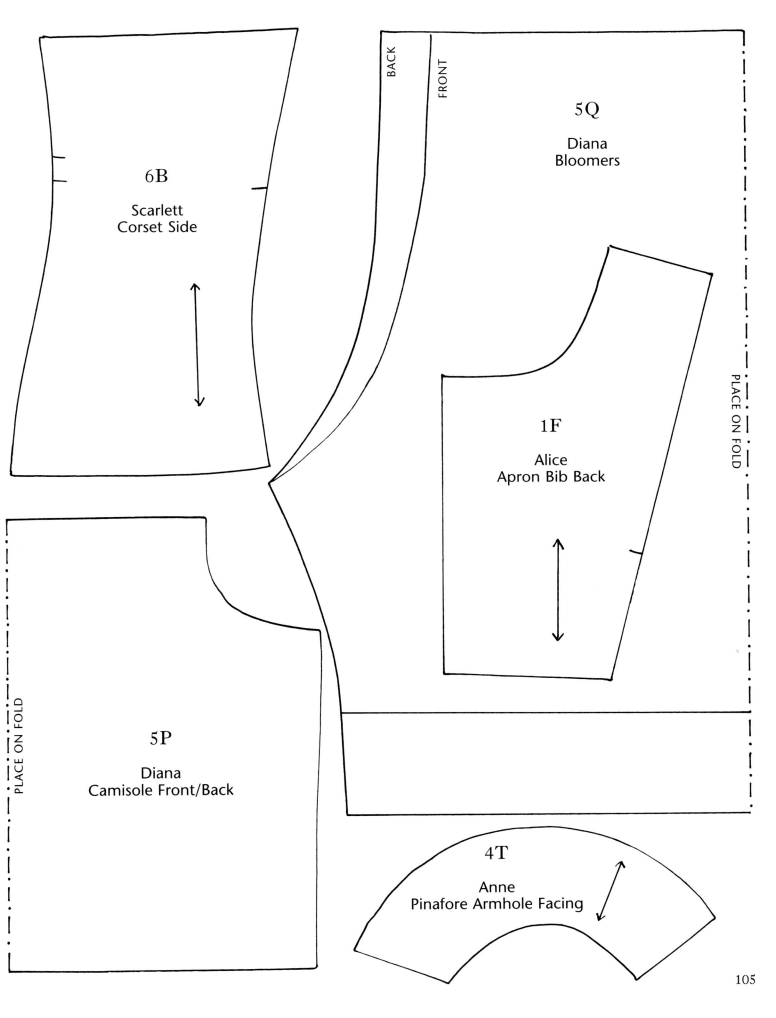

6B

Scarlett
Corset Side

5Q

Diana
Bloomers

BACK

FRONT

PLACE ON FOLD

1F

Alice
Apron Bib Back

PLACE ON FOLD

5P

Diana
Camisole Front/Back

4T

Anne
Pinafore Armhole Facing

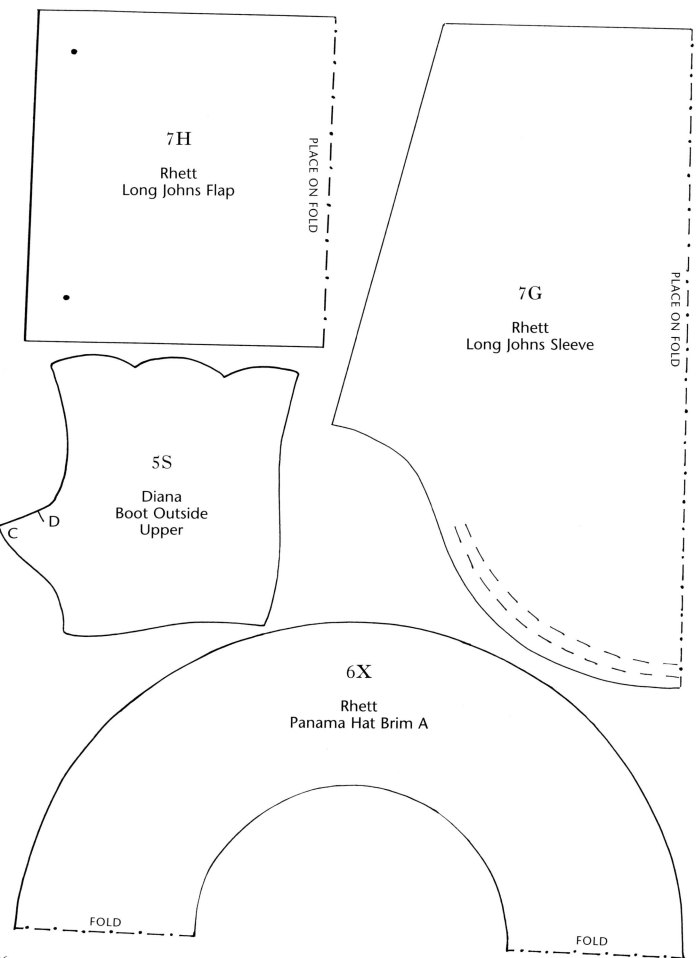

7H

Rhett
Long Johns Flap

PLACE ON FOLD

7G

Rhett
Long Johns Sleeve

PLACE ON FOLD

5S

Diana
Boot Outside
Upper

D

C

6X

Rhett
Panama Hat Brim A

FOLD

FOLD

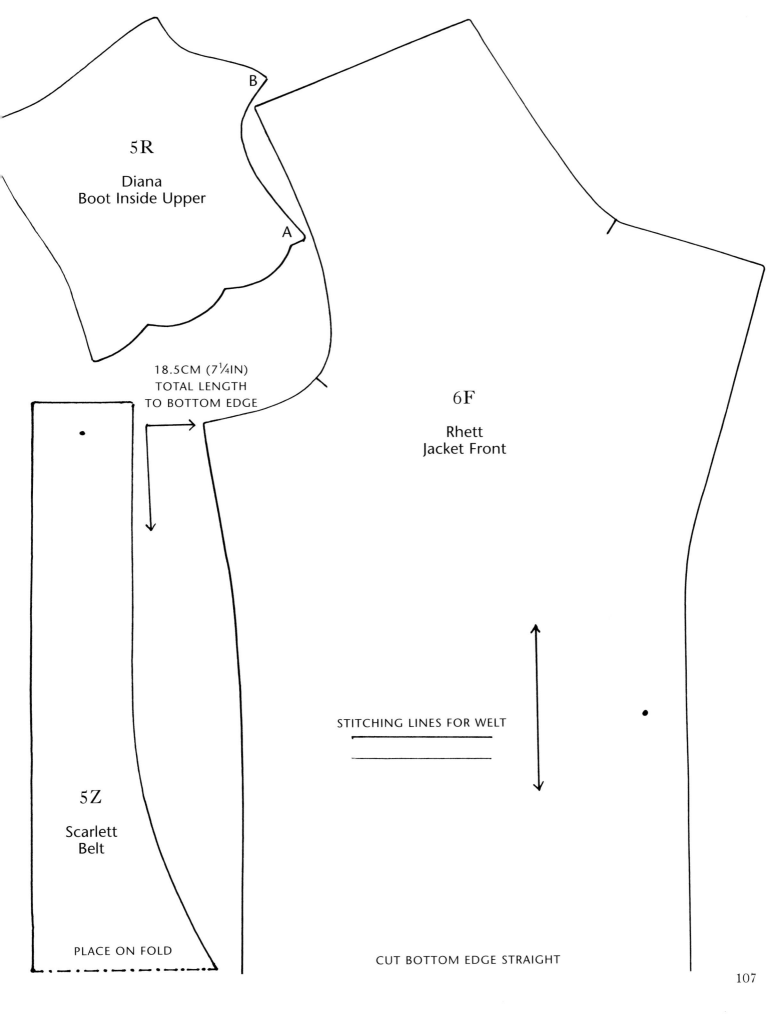

5R

Diana
Boot Inside Upper

B

A

18.5CM (7¼IN)
TOTAL LENGTH
TO BOTTOM EDGE

6F

Rhett
Jacket Front

5Z

Scarlett
Belt

STITCHING LINES FOR WELT

PLACE ON FOLD

CUT BOTTOM EDGE STRAIGHT

107

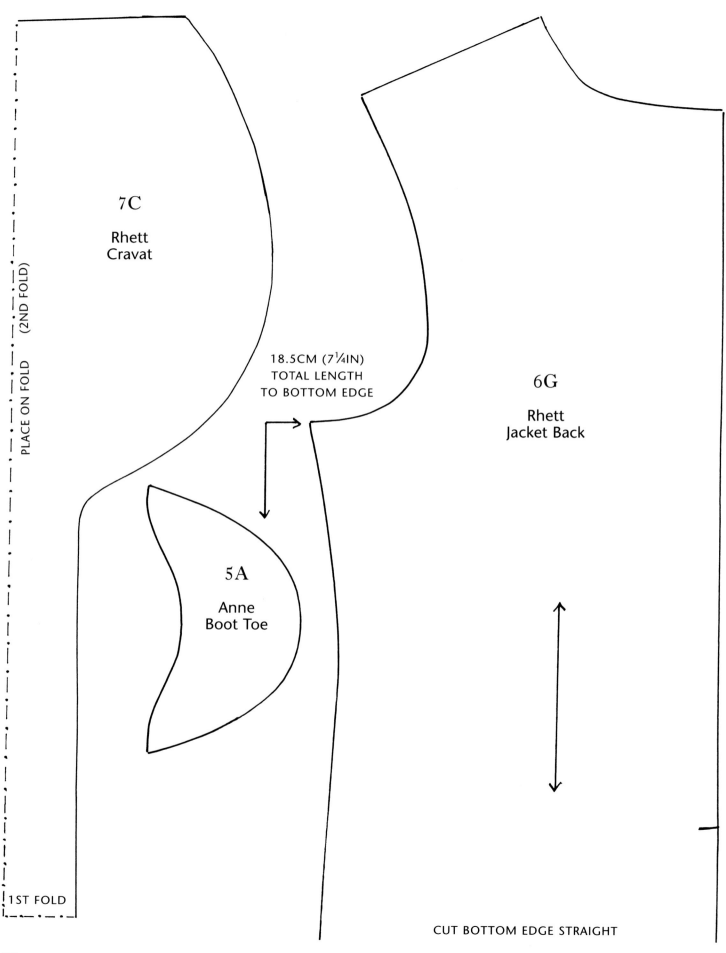

PLACE ON FOLD (2ND FOLD)

7C

Rhett
Cravat

18.5CM (7¼IN)
TOTAL LENGTH
TO BOTTOM EDGE

6G

Rhett
Jacket Back

5A

Anne
Boot Toe

1ST FOLD

CUT BOTTOM EDGE STRAIGHT

108

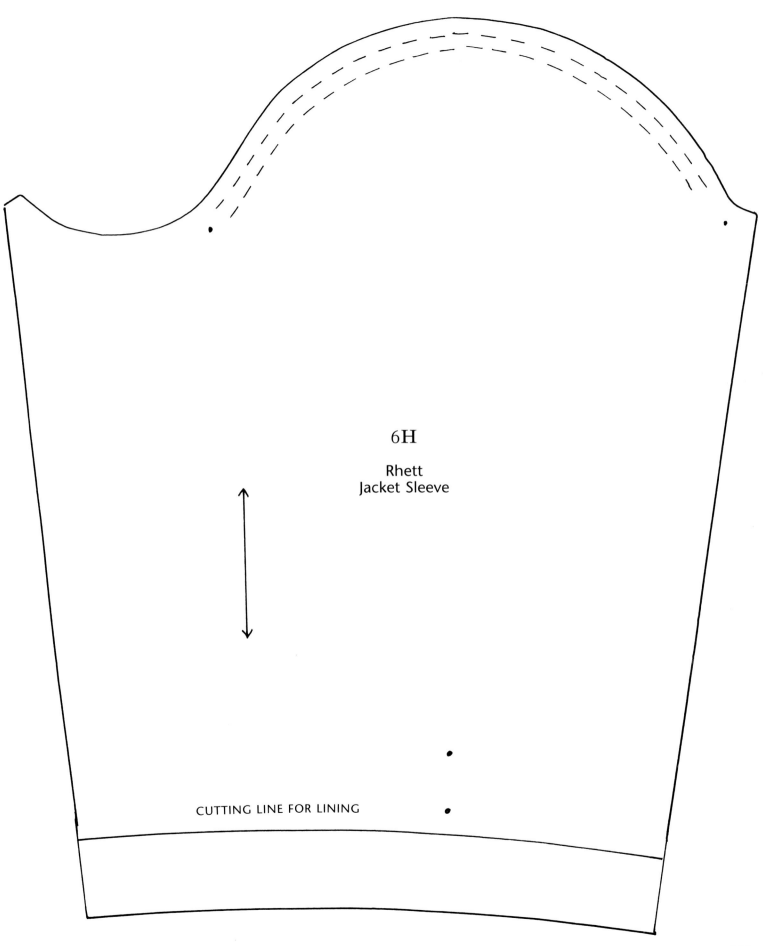

6H

Rhett
Jacket Sleeve

CUTTING LINE FOR LINING

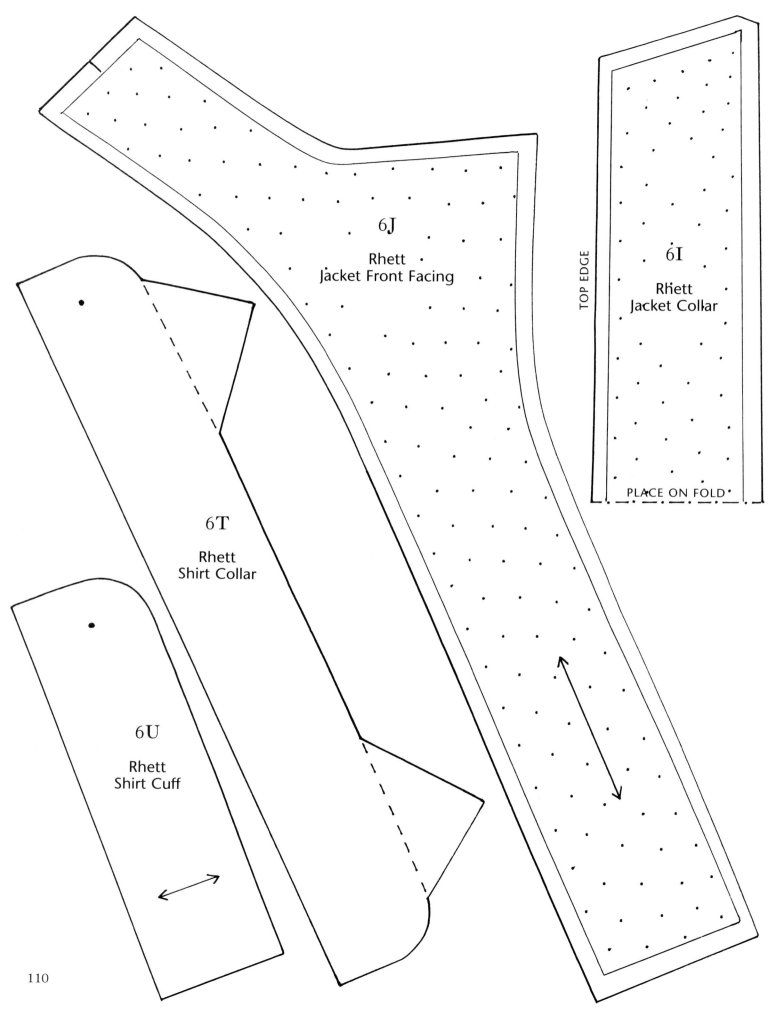

6J

Rhett
Jacket Front Facing

6I

Rhett
Jacket Collar

TOP EDGE

PLACE ON FOLD

6T

Rhett
Shirt Collar

6U

Rhett
Shirt Cuff

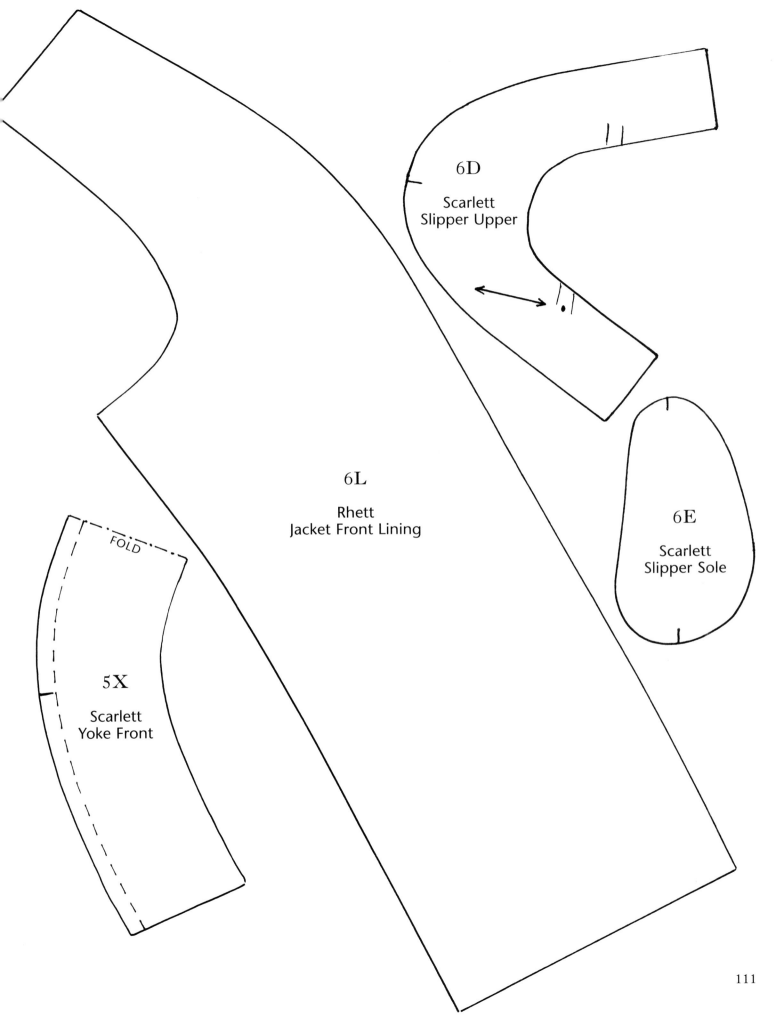

6D

Scarlett
Slipper Upper

6L

Rhett
Jacket Front Lining

6E

Scarlett
Slipper Sole

FOLD

5X

Scarlett
Yoke Front

111

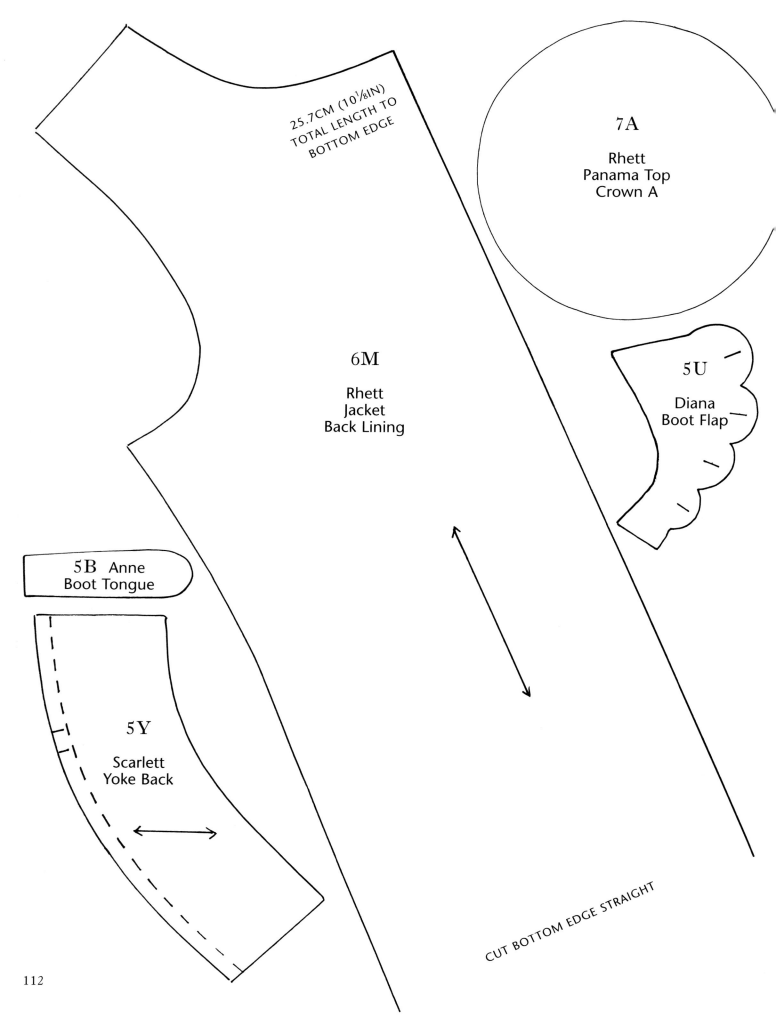

25.7CM (10⅛IN)
TOTAL LENGTH TO
BOTTOM EDGE

7A

Rhett
Panama Top
Crown A

6M

Rhett
Jacket
Back Lining

5U

Diana
Boot Flap

5B Anne
Boot Tongue

5Y

Scarlett
Yoke Back

CUT BOTTOM EDGE STRAIGHT

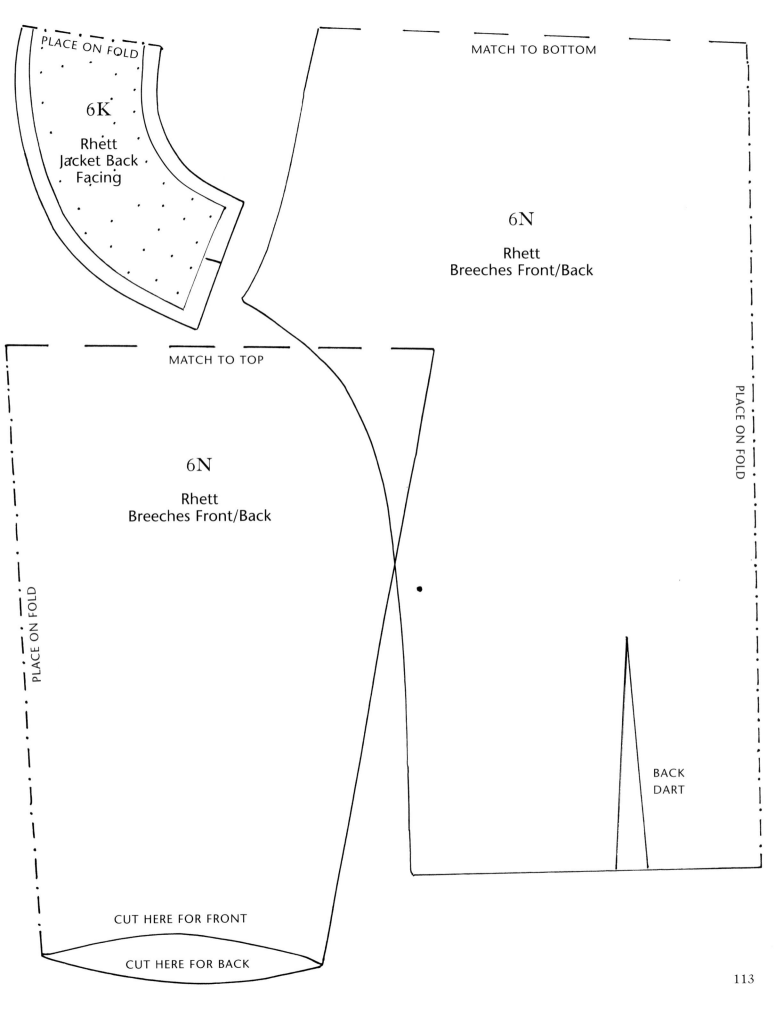

PLACE ON FOLD

6K

Rhett
Jacket Back
Facing

MATCH TO BOTTOM

6N

Rhett
Breeches Front/Back

MATCH TO TOP

PLACE ON FOLD

PLACE ON FOLD

6N

Rhett
Breeches Front/Back

BACK
DART

CUT HERE FOR FRONT

CUT HERE FOR BACK

113

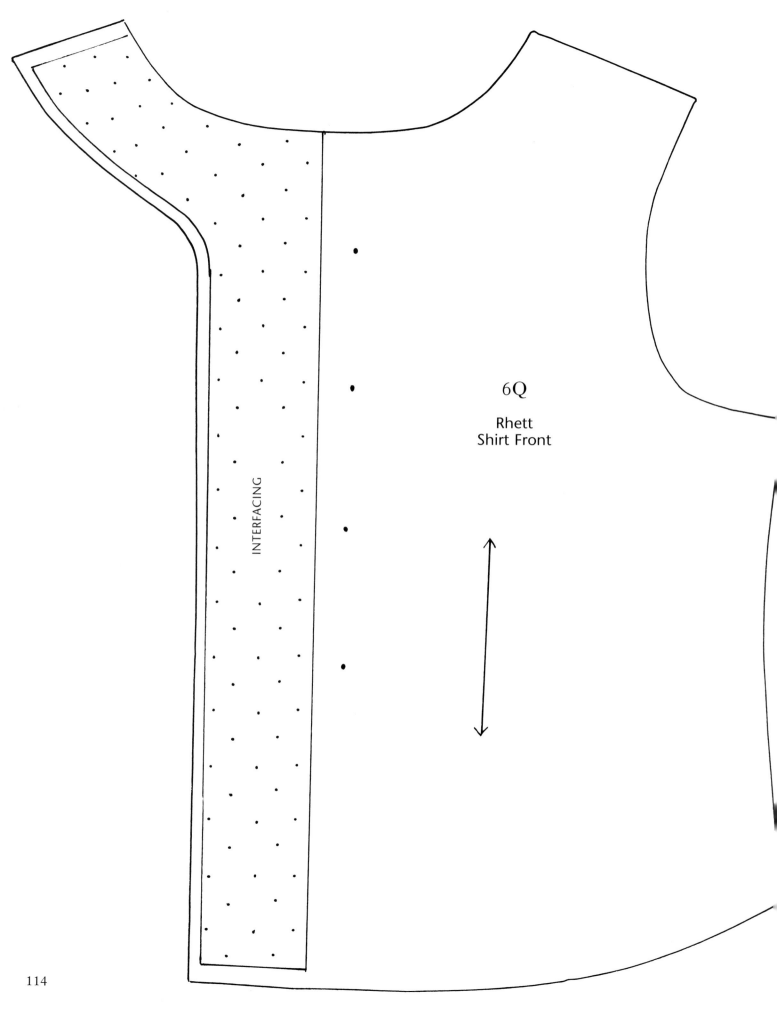

INTERFACING

6Q

Rhett
Shirt Front

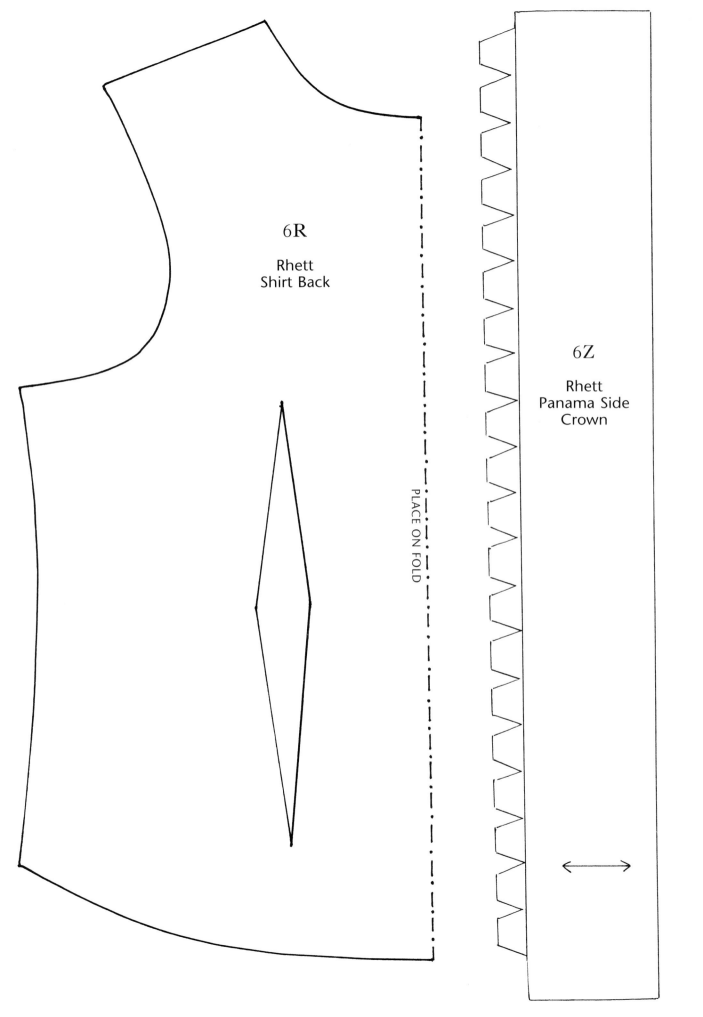

6R

Rhett
Shirt Back

PLACE ON FOLD

6Z

Rhett
Panama Side
Crown

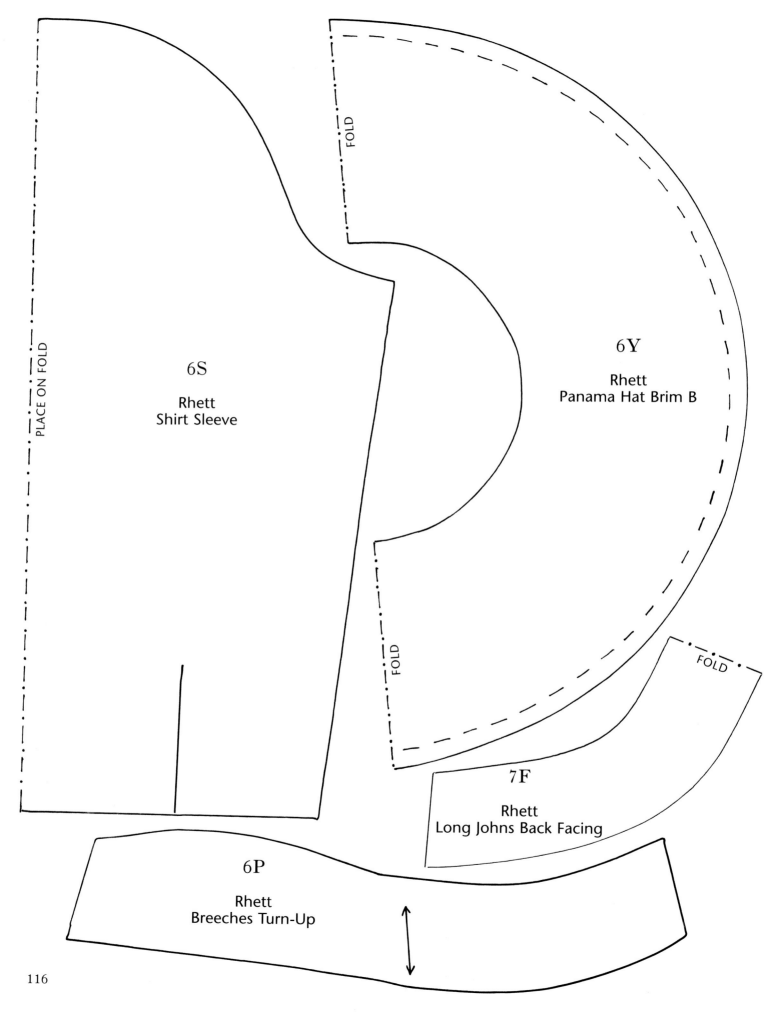

PLACE ON FOLD

FOLD

6S

Rhett
Shirt Sleeve

6Y

Rhett
Panama Hat Brim B

FOLD

FOLD

7F

Rhett
Long Johns Back Facing

6P

Rhett
Breeches Turn-Up

116

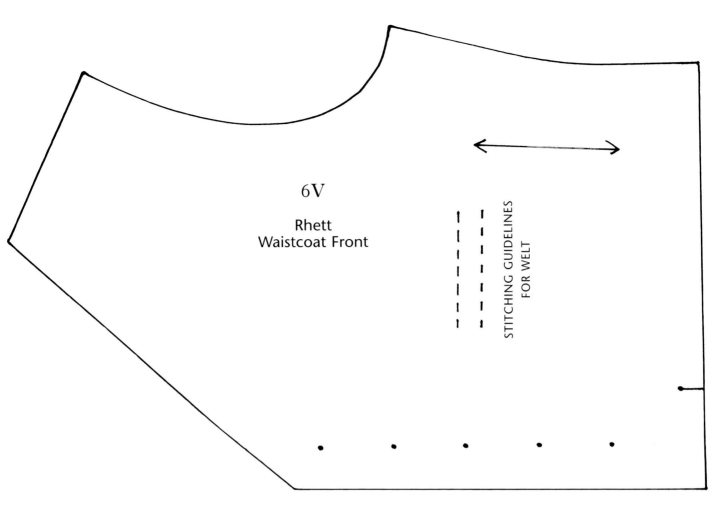

6V

Rhett
Waistcoat Front

STITCHING GUIDELINES FOR WELT

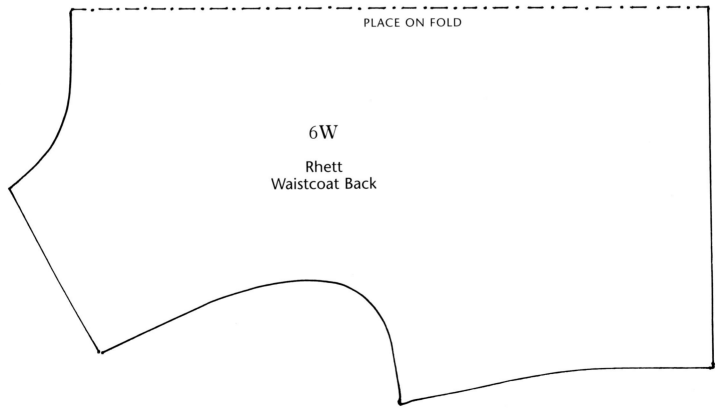

PLACE ON FOLD

6W

Rhett
Waistcoat Back

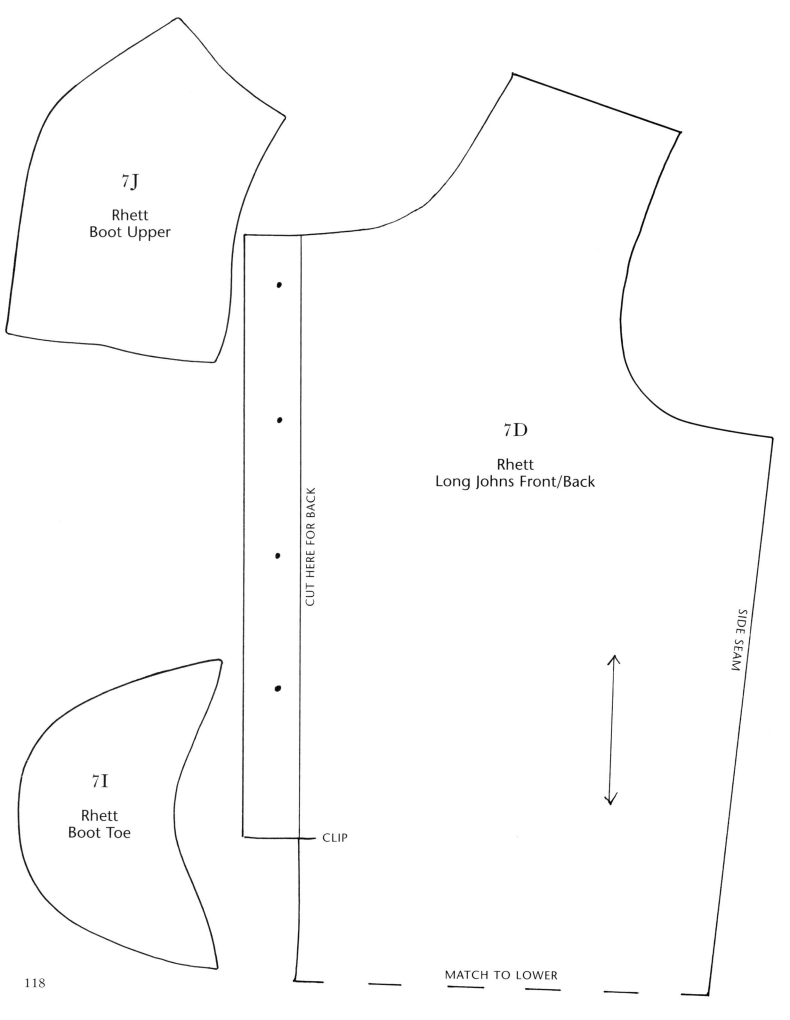

7J

Rhett
Boot Upper

CUT HERE FOR BACK

7D

Rhett
Long Johns Front/Back

SIDE SEAM

CLIP

7I

Rhett
Boot Toe

118

MATCH TO LOWER

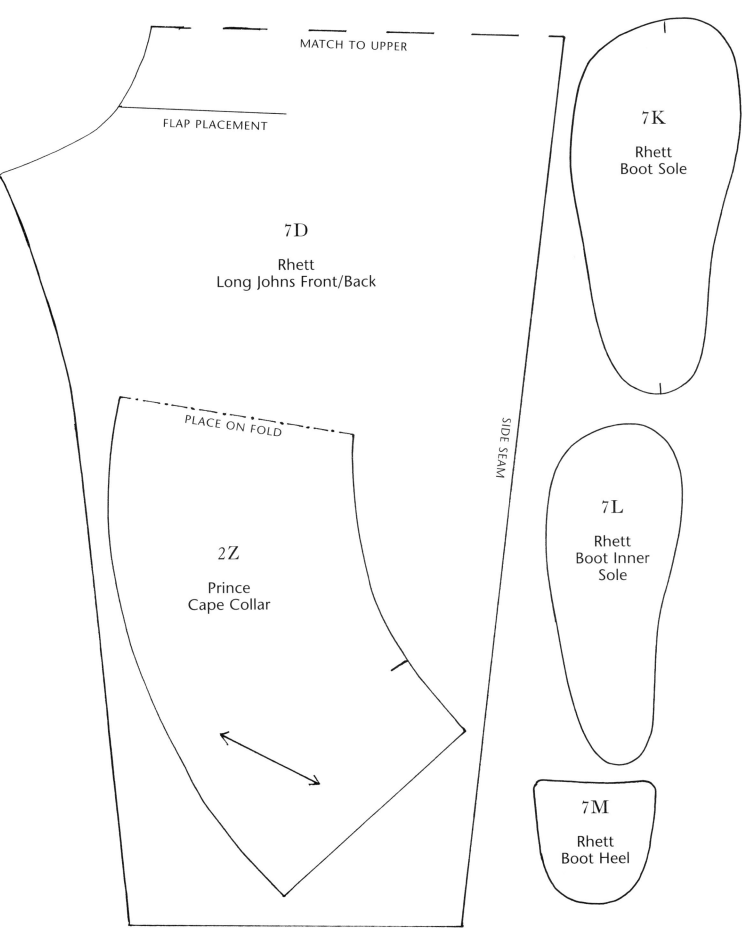

MATCH TO UPPER

FLAP PLACEMENT

7D

Rhett
Long Johns Front/Back

7K

Rhett
Boot Sole

PLACE ON FOLD

2Z

Prince
Cape Collar

SIDE SEAM

7L

Rhett
Boot Inner
Sole

7M

Rhett
Boot Heel

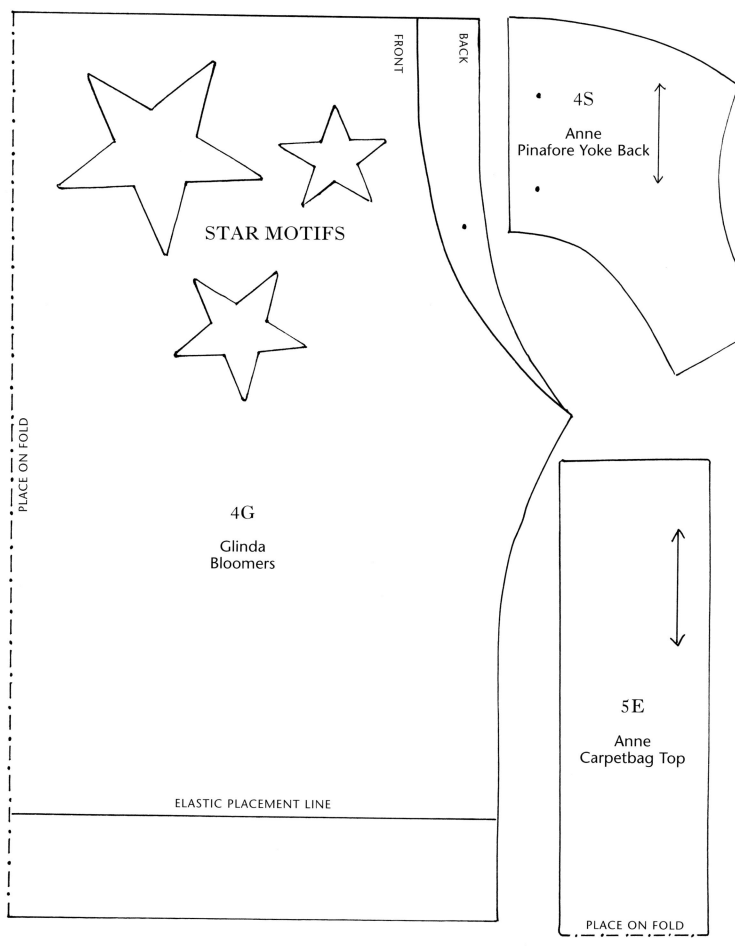

STAR MOTIFS

FRONT

BACK

PLACE ON FOLD

4G

Glinda
Bloomers

ELASTIC PLACEMENT LINE

4S

Anne
Pinafore Yoke Back

5E

Anne
Carpetbag Top

PLACE ON FOLD

Suppliers

Ellie's Doll Workshop
1526 Wimborne Road
Kinson, Bournemouth
Dorset, BH11 9AF, UK
tel: 01202 572626
email: mike@elliesdolls.freeserve.co.uk
www.elliesdolls.co.uk

Recollect Studios
17 Junction Road
Burgess Hill
West Sussex, RH15 0HG, UK
tel/fax: 01444 871052
email: dollshopuk@aol.com

Acknowledgments

I would like to thank everyone at David & Charles
for all their help in producing *The Dolls' Clothes
Storybook Collection*, in particular Executive Editor,
Cheryl Brown for her help and encouragement,
to Prudence Rogers for her artistic layouts and
wonderful background designs, to Ame Verso and
to Joan Gubbin for their humour in deciphering
my text, and a special thanks to photographer,
Ginette Chapman whose professionalism and eye
for detail have helped to create a beautiful book.

I would also like to thank Rosemary Wallis for
creating 'Toto', the lovely little Cairn terrier who
accompanies Dorothy. For more about
Rosemary's dogs, you can contact her at:
Vieto, 73 Botley Road, Swanwick, Southampton
SO31 1AZ, UK Tel: 01489 582005

The Author

Christina Harris was a keen needlewoman from an
early age, making clothes for her dolls before
progressing to her own. After undertaking a degree in
photography, Christina became a designer and maker of
teddy bears, producing bears for collectors and shops
in the UK, America, Switzerland and Japan. She has
contributed teddy bear clothes patterns and articles to
a large number of magazines including *Teddy Bear Club
International*, *Teddy Bear Times Japan* and *Crafts Beautiful*.
Since revisiting dolls' clothing, Christina has enjoyed
considerable success, writing *The Dolls' Clothes Storybook
Collection* as a follow up to her popular book *The Dolls'
Clothes Collection*, also published by David & Charles.
She also continues to make full size clothes, and
recently dressed both the bride and the bridesmaids at
her daughter's wedding. Christina lives with her husband
David in East Sussex.

Index